Canada Dept. of Customs

# Customs and Excise Tariff with List of Warehousing Ports in the Dominion

Sterling exchange & franc tables, compiled from official sources, 21st

February, 1877

Canada Dept. of Customs

**Customs and Excise Tariff with List of Warehousing Ports in the Dominion**
*Sterling exchange & franc tables, compiled from official sources, 21st February, 1877*

ISBN/EAN: 9783337119881

Printed in Europe, USA, Canada, Australia, Japan

Cover: Foto ©Suzi / pixelio.de

More available books at **www.hansebooks.com**

# CUSTOMS

### AND

# EXCISE TARIFF,

#### WITH

## LIST OF WAREHOUSING PORTS IN THE DOMINION,

## STERLING EXCHANGE & FRANC TABLES

#### COMPILED FROM OFFICIAL SOURCES,

*21st February, 1877.*

𝕸ontreal :

DAWSON BROTHERS, PUBLISHERS.

1877.

# CUSTOMS TARIFF

*As in force since February 21st, 1877.*

## A

P. C.

| | |
|---|---|
| Acid—Acetic and Vinegar........12 cents per Imp. gal ; | |
| pkgs............................................ | 17½ |
| Acid—Sulphuric................ ½ cent per lb. ; pkgs. | 17½ |
| Acids of every description, except Acetic Acid, Vinegar, | |
| and Sulphuric Acid.............................. | Free |
| Advertising Pamphlets............................. | 5 |
| Agricultural Societies' Farming Utensils and Implements, | |
| when imported by, for the encouragement of Agricul- | |
| ture ........................................... | Free |
| Alabaster, &c.—see Fancy Goods.................... | 17½ |
| Alcohol................$1.20 per Imp. gal. ; pkgs. | 17½ |
| Ale, Beer and Porter in casks....12 cents per Imp. gal. ; | |
| pkgs ......................................... | 17½ |
| Do. in bottles...........18 cents per Imp. gal. ; pkgs. | 17½ |
| Almonds ........................................ | 17½ |
| Alum........................................... | Free |
| Aniline Salts, for dyeing purposes.................. | Free |
| Agricultural Implements, not elsewhere specified ...... | 17½ |
| Annato—Liquid or Solid ......................... | Free |
| Anatomical Preparations.......................... | Free |
| Anchors ....................................... | Free |
| Angola Hair, unmanufactured...................... | Free |
| Animals—Horned Cattle........................... | 10 |
| "        Horses ............................... | 10 |
| "        Sheep ............................... | 10 |
| "        Swine............................... | 10 |
| "        All others ........................... | 10 |

p. c

| | |
|---|---|
| Beer in wood............12 cents per Imp. gal.; pkgs. | 17½ |
| Beer in bottles...........18   "       "       " | 17½ |
| Belting and Hose Duck............................... | Free |
| Berries, used chiefly in Dyeing...................... | Free |
| Bitters, containing Spirits.......1.80 per Imp. gal; pkgs. | 17½ |
| Blacking ........................................... | 17½ |
| Black Lead ......................................... | 17½ |
| Baking Powders .................................... | 17½ |
| Bath Bricks ....................................... | 17½ |
| Biscuit ........................................... | 17½ |
| Biscuit and Bread, produce of Great Britain and New-foundland ........................................ | Free |
| Blacking for Military .............................. | Free |
| Bicarbonate of Soda ............................... | 17½ |
| Bleaching Powders................................. | Free |
| Bichromate of Potash .............................. | Free |
| Books, being reprint of British Copyright Works ....... | 12½ |
| Books, Blank Account and Copy Books, to be written or drawn upon .................................... | 17½ |
| Books, Periodicals and Pamphlets printed, not being reprint of British Copyright Works, nor Blank Account-Books, nor Copy Books, nor books to be written in or drawn upon, nor reprints of Books printed in Canada, nor printed Sheet Music.................. | 5 |
| Book-binders' Tools and Implements................. | Free |
| "       Mill Boards...................... | Free |
| "       Cloth ........................ | Free |
| Boots and Shoes (Leather).......................... | 17½ |
| Boot Felt, and Felt for Hats and Gloves.............. | 10 |
| Book, Map and News Printing Paper ................. | 17½ |
| Bone, manufactures of.  (See Fancy Goods.) .......... | 17½ |
| Bonnets, Hats and Caps ........................... | 17½ |
| Beads and Bead Ornaments.  (See Fancy Goods) ....... | 17½ |
| Blankets, Woollen ................................. | 17½ |
| Bibles, Testaments and Devotional Books ............ | 5 |
| Binnacle Lamps ................................... | 5 |

P. C.

| | |
|---|---|
| Boiler, Plate Iron ..................................... | 5 |
| Bolting Cloth........................................... | Free |
| Borax.................................................. | Free |
| Boot and Shoe Making Machines ...................... | 17½ |
| Bone Crushers and parts thereof...................... | 17½ |
| Botanical Specimens................................... | Free |
| Bracelets, Braids, &c., made of Hair.................. | 17½ |
| Boxes (Fancy), Ornamental Cases & Writing Desks ..... | 17½ |
| Bran .................................................. | 10 |
| Bran from B.N.A. Provinces........................... | Free |
| Brandy ...................$1.20 per Imp. gal.; pkgs.. | 17½ |
| Brass and Copper, manufactured ...................... | 17½ |
| Brass, in bars, rods, sheets and strips ............... | Free |
| Brass and Iron Tubes and Piping, when drawn.......... | 17½ |
| Brass and Iron Tubes and Piping, when drawn or otherwise ............................................. | 17½ |
| Brass or Copper Wire, and Wire Cloth ................ | Free |
| Brass in scraps....................................... | Free |
| Blue Black and Chinese Blue .......................... | Free |
| Brass and Tin Clasps, Slides and Spangles, for the manufacture of Hoop Skirts ............................... | Free |
| Brimstone, Roll or Flour.............................. | Free |
| Bristles and Hog's Hair of all kinds .................. | Free |
| Britannia and Metal Ware............................. | 17½ |
| Brooms and Brushes of all kinds ..................... | 17½ |
| Broom Corn........................................... | Free |
| Buckwheat............................................ | Free |
| Bulbs, other than Medicinal........................... | Free |
| Bullion and Coin, except U.S. Silver Coin ............ | Free |
| Burrstones ............................................ | Free |
| Busts, natural size, not being Cast, or produced by any mechanical process ................................. | Free |
| Butter.......................4 cents per lb.; pkgs. | 17½ |
| Butter from B.N.A. Provinces......................... | Free |
| Bunting, for Ships.................................... | 5 |
| Bark—Tanners' ...................................... | Free |

p. c.

Blocks, and Patent Bushes for Ships' Blocks ............ 5
Bronze Ornaments....... ...... ............. ........ 17½
British Gum ...................................... Free

## C

Cabinets of Coins, Antiquities, Gems and Medals........ Free
Cables, Iron Chain (Ships'), over one-half of an inch,
    shackled or swiveled, or not .................... Free
Cables, Hemp (Ship's materials) ......... ............. 5
    "   Grass (   "    "  ) .................... 5
Cabinet Ware or Furniture ....................... 17½
Carbolic or Heavy Oil, used in the manufacture of Wood
    Block Pavements, &c........................... Free
Carboys, containing Sulphuric Acid .................. 17½
Cards, Playing ................................. 25
Candles and Tapers of Tallow, Wax, or any other material 17½
Canada Plates, Tinned Plates, Sheet Iron.............. 5
Cane Juice, Syrups, &c...⅜ths of 1 cent per lb. and *ad val.* 25
Caoutchouc, or India Rubber, and Gutta Percha, unmanu-
    factured.... ........ ............................ Free
Canvas, for Ships...... ........................... 5
Canvas, for manufacture of Floor Oil Cloths, not less than
    18 feet wide, and not pressed or calendered......... Free
Canvas, when otherwise used....................... 17½
Caps, Hats and Bonnets .......................... 17½
Carriages ....................................... 17½
Carriages of Travellers, and Carriages laden with Merchan-
    dise, Hawkers and Circus Troupes excepted........ Free
Carpets and Hearth Rugs.......................... 17½
Cashmere ...................................... 17½
Cassia, ground ................................. 25
    "   unground............................... 17½
Castile Soap ................................... 17½
Casts as Models for the use of Schools of Design........ Free
Castings, Iron, all others......................... 17½

P. C.

| | |
|---|---|
| Cement, Marine or Hydraulic, unground................ | Free |
| Cement, Hydraulic, ground and calcined............... | 17½ |
| Chairs, Wrought Iron or Steel, imported for Railway purposes.. ...................................... | Free |
| Cheese..................3 cents per lb. ; pkgs. | 17½ |
| Cheese Vats, Presses and Factory Heaters, and parts thereof............................. | 17½ |
| Cheese, produce of Newfoundland.................... | Free |
| Chandeliers, Girondoles and Gas Fittings............. | 17½ |
| Chinaware, Earthenware and Crockery............... | 17½ |
| Charts, Maps and Atlasses.......................... | 17½ |
| Charitable Institutions, donations of Clothing for....... | Free |
| Church Bells...................................... | Free |
| Chaff Cutters, and parts thereof.................... | 17½ |
| Churns .......................................... | 17½ |
| Chicory or other Root, or Vegetable used as Coffee, raw or green ...................3 cents per lb. | |
| Chicory, kiln-dried, roasted or ground ....4 cents per lb. | |
| Cider............................................ | 17½ |
| Cigars .........................50 cents per lb. and | 20 |
| Cigarettes....................50 cents per lb. and | 20 |
| Cinnamon, ground................................. | 25 |
| "          unground............................... | 17½ |
| Citrons, Green................................... | 10 |
| Citrons imported in brine for the purpose of being candied | Free |
| Clay, Earth, Sand and Pipe Clay.................... | Free |
| Coach and Harness Furniture ...................... | 17½ |
| Coal............................................. | Free |
| Coke ............................................ | Free |
| Coal from Newfoundland........................... | Free |
| Coke from Newfoundland........................... | Free |
| Cocoa, Bean and Shell............................. | Free |
| Cocoa and Chocolate, not sweetened................. | 17½ |
| "      "      "      sweetened.......1 cent per lb. and | 25 |
| Cocoa Nut Oils in their natural state................ | Free |
| Cocoa Nuts ...................................... | 10 |

P. C.

Cocoa Paste, from Great Britain and B N.A. Provinces...        Free
Cologne Water and Perfumed Spirits, not in flasks..$1.80
  per Imp. gal.; pkgs..............................        17½
Cologne Water and Perfumed Spirits, in flasks or bottles,
  not weighing more than four ounces................        25
Communion Plate.......................................        Free
Composition Spikes and Nails..........................        Free
Compasses, Ships'.....................................        5
Coffee, Green....................2 cents per lb.; pkgs.        17½
Coffee, Roasted.................3 cents per lb.: pkgs.        17½
Clocks................................................        17½
Clothing or Wearing Apparel...........................        17½
Clothing for Army and Navy, or donations of, for Charit-
  able Institutions..................................        Free
Collar Cloth Paper....................................        Free
Commissariat Stores...................................        Free
Colors, &c., viz.: Lakes in pulp, Scarlet, Maroon, Ultra-
  marine, Chinese Blue, Raw Umber; Blue, Black,
  Paris and Permanent Greens, Satin, and fine Washed
  White, Bi-chromate of Potash, Sugar of Lead and
  British Gum........................................        Free
Confectionery...............1 cent per lb., and ad val.        25
Copper Tubes and Pipings.....................    "        17½
Copper in pigs, bars, rods, bolts, or sheets and sheathing.        Free
Copper or Brass, manufactured.........................        17½
Corkwood, or the Bark of the Corkwood Tree............        Free
Copper Pipes, drawn...................................        17½
Cordage for Ship's use................................        5
Cordials.................$1.80 per Imp. gal.; pkgs.        17½
Cottons, viz.:
   "   Bleached and Unbleached....................        17½
   "   Printed, Painted or Colored................        17½
   "   Ginghams and Plaids.......................        17½
   "   Jeans, Denims and Drillings...............        17½
   "   Clothing or Wearing Apparel...............        17½
   "   All others................................        17½

P. C.

| | |
|---|---|
| Cotton Thread, in hanks, No. 6 ply, white, not under No. 20 yarn | 10 |
| Cotton Thread, on spools or hanks | 17½ |
| Cotton Yarn and Cotton Twist | 17½ |
| Cotton Warp, not coarser than No. 40 | 17½ |
| Corn, Indian | Free |
| Cotton Waste | Free |
| Cotton Wool | Free |
| Cotton Candle Wick | Free |
| Cotton and Flax Waste | Free |
| Cotton Netting and Woollen Netting, for India Rubber Shoes and Gloves | 10 |
| Cordage—Ropes not elsewhere specified | 17½ |
| Cordage—Twines | 17½ |
| Corks | 17½ |
| Corn Huskers | 17½ |
| Cranks, for Steamboats, forged in the rough | Free |
| "    for Mills,    "    "    " | Free |
| Coin and Bullion, except U.S. Silver Coin | Free |
| Coin (Silver) of U.S. | 17½ |
| Cream of Tartar, in Crystals | Free |
| Currants, Dried | 17½ |
| Curled Hair, used in the manufacture of Sofas, Mattrasses, &c. | Free |
| Cultivators, and parts thereof | 17½ |
| Cutlery | 17½ |

## D

| | |
|---|---|
| Dead Eyes, Ships' | 5 |
| Dead Lights, " | 5 |
| Deck Plugs, " | 5 |
| Diamonds and Precious Stones, unset | Free |
| Dried Fruits and Nuts of all kinds, viz. : | |
| "    Currants | 17½ |
| "    Dates | 17½ |

P. C.

| | |
|---|---|
| Engines—Steam Fire | 17½ |
| "     Locomotives | 17½ |
| "     Others | 17½ |
| "     Locomotive Frames | 10 |
| "     Axles for Locomotives | 10 |
| "     Hoop Iron, or Steel, for tires of wheels, bent and welded | 10 |
| "     Cranks and Crank Axles | 10 |
| "     Crank Pins and Connecting Rods | 10 |
| "     Piston Rods, Guide and Slide Bars | 10 |
| Essences, not containing any Spirits | 17½ |
| "     containing Spirits ..$1.80 per Imp. gal. ; pkgs. | 17½ |
| Extracts, mixed with Spirits or Strong Waters, $1.80 " | 17½ |

## F

| | |
|---|---|
| Factory Heaters, Cheese Vats, Presses, &c | 17½ |
| Factory and Mill Machinery | 17½ |
| Fancy Goods, viz.: | |
| "     Alabaster, Spar, Bronze, Terra Cotta or Composition Ornaments | 17½ |
| "     Articles embroidered with Gold, Silver or other Metals | 17½ |
| "     Bracelets, Braids, &c., made of Hair | 17½ |
| "     Beads and Bead Ornaments | 17½ |
| "     Boxes (Fancy), Ornamental Cases and Writing Desks | 17½ |
| "     Combs, and manufactures of Bone, Shell, Horn and Ivory | 17½ |
| "     Coral, cut or manufactured | 17½ |
| "     Dolls | 17½ |
| "     Fans and Fire Screens | 17½ |
| "     Feathers and Flowers, artificial and ornamental | 17½ |
| "     Gold and Silver Cloths, Tassels, Thread, &c... | 17½ |
| "     Ivory or Bone Dice, Draughts, Chessmen, &c.. | 17½ |
| "     Millinery of all kinds | 17½ |

| P. C. | | P. C. |
|---|---|---|
| 17½ | Fancy Goods, viz. : | |
| 17½ |     "   Pearl, Composition, and manufactures of...... | 17½ |
| 17½ |     "   Thread, Lace and Insertions.............. ...... | 17½ |
| 10 | Fancy Straw Plaits, Tuscan and Grass................ | Free |
| 10 | Farming Implements & Utensils, when imported by Agricultural Societies for encouragement of Agriculture.. | Free |
| 10 | Felt for Hats, Boots and Gloves ..................... | 10 |
| 10 | Felt Hats.......................................... | 17½ |
| 10 | Felt, others not elsewhere specified.................,...... | 17½ |
| 10 | Felt for Roofing.... ................................ | 17½ |
| 17½ | Fibrilla, Mexican Fibre or Tampico, White or Black, and | |
| 17½ |     other vegetable fibres for manufacture ........... | Free |
| 17½ | Filberts. (See Dried Nuts.).... ..................... | 17½ |
| | Figs. (See Dried Fruits.)............ .............. | 17½ |
| | Files. (See Manufactures.)...................... ..... | 17½ |
| | Fire Arms of all kinds. (See Guns.) When from United | |
| 17½ |     States, entry must be authorized by Department.... | 17½ |
| 17½ | Fire Brick, common...........,................. ...... | Free |
| | Fire Brick, shaped................................. | 17½ |
| | Fire Clay......................................... | Free |
| 17½ | Firewood.......................................... | Free |
| | Fire Works....................................... | 17½ |
| 17½ | Fire Engines—Steam................................. | 17½ |
| 17½ |     "      Other ...................... ........ | 17½ |
| 17½ | Fire Extinguishers—Chemical...................... | 17½ |
| | Fish Plates. (See Railroad.)........ ............... | Free |
| 17½ | Fish from U.S , including Cod, Haddock & Pollock, fresh. | Free |
| |     "     "     "     "     " . dry salted...... | Free |
| 17½ |     "     "     "     "     " wet salted .... | Free |
| 17½ |     "     "     "     "     " pickled ....... | Free |
| 17½ |     "     "     "     "     " smoked........ | Free |
| 17½ |     " Mackerel, fresh ..................,............ | Free |
| 17½ |     "     "    pickled ..... .................... | Free |
| 17½ |     " Halibut, fresh................................ | Free |
| 17½ |     "     " pickled .............................. | Free |
| 17½ |     " Herrings, fresh ............................. | Free |

P. C.

| | |
|---|---|
| Fish—Herrings, pickled........................ ..... ...... | Free |
| "       "       smoked............................. | Free |
| "   Sea Fish, other, fresh........................... | Free |
| "       "       "   pickled.... .................... | Free |
| "       "       "   preserved ..................... | Free |
| "   Oysters, fresh in shell.......................... | Free |
| "       "   fresh in cans....................... | Free |
| "       "   shelled, in bulk..................... | Free |
| "   Lobsters, fresh ...... ......................... | Free |
| "       "   preserved, in cans................... | Free |
| "   Bait Fish ..................................... | Free |
| "   "   Clams or other........................... | Free |
| "   from United States—Salmon, fresh............... | Free |
| "   "   "   "   smoked ............ | Free |
| "   "   "   "   canned ........... | Free |
| "   "   "   "   pickled ............. | Free |
| "   "   "   All other, fresh............. | Free |
| "   "   "   "   pickled........... | Free |
| "   "   "   Fish Oil, Whale............. | Free |
| "   "   "   "   Cod ................ | Free |
| "   "   "   "   others, free ........ | Free |
| "   and products of Fish and Fish Oil, when the products of Newfoundland ........................... | Free |
| Fish, salted or smoked, from all other Countries...1 cent per lb. ; pkgs.............. ................ .... | 17½ |
| Fish, preserved, except from U.S. and B.N.A. Provinces.. | 17½ |
| Fishing Nets and Seines........................... | Free |
| Fish Hooks, Lines and Fish Twines ................. | Free |
| Flat Wire for Crinoline, uncovered................... | Free |
| Flax Waste..................................... | Free |
| Flax, Hemp and Tow, undressed .................... | Free |
| Flax Seed...................................... | Free |
| Flour of Wheat or Rye.   (See Grain.).................. | Free |
| Flour and Meal of any other Grain................... | Free |
| Flour, the produce of Newfoundland.................. | Free |
| Flannels.   (See Woollens.)........................ | 17½ |

| P. C. | | P. C. |
|---|---|---|
| Free | Fruits, Green of all kinds, viz : | |
| Free | " Apples and Pears...... ........................ | 10 |
| Free | " Grapes...... ........ ...... ...... ......... | 10 |
| Free | " Lemons and Oranges ...................... | 10 |
| Free | " Peaches .... ...... ...... ...... ........... | 10 |
| Free | " Pine Apples....... ...... ...... ......... | 10 |
| Free | " All others, not elsewhere specified.............. | 10 |
| Free | " Green and Dried, from B.N. A. Provinces......... | Free |
| Free | Fruits preserved in Brandy or other Spirits....$1.80 per | |
| Free | Imp. gal. ; pkgs...... ...... ...... ......... | 17½ |
| Free | Furs, Skins, Felts or Tails, undressed.................. | Free |
| Free | Furs. (See Manufactures.) ...................... ..... | 17½ |
| Free | Furs or Skins, the products of Fish or Marine Animals .. | Free |
| Free | Frogs. (See Railroad.) ............. ...... ............ | Free |
| Free | Furniture or Cabinet Ware......................... | 17½ |
| Free | " for Coaches and Harness. .................. | 17½ |
| Free | | |
| Free | | |
| Free | | |
| Free | **G** | |
| Free | Galvanized Iron. (See Iron, &c.)..................... | 5 |
| Free | Galvanized Wire, except for Wire Rigging for Ships..... | 5 |
| | Gas Fittings...... ...... ...... ......... ......... .... | 17½ |
| Free | Gelatine ...... ...... ...... ...... ...... ...... ...... | 17½ |
| | Gems and Medals, Cabinets of.................... ...... | Free |
| 17½ | German Plated & Gilded Ware, manufactured. of all kinds | 17½ |
| 17½ | Gin, including Geneva and Old Tom, $1.20 per Imp. gal. ; | |
| Free | pkgs..... ...... ...... ...... | 17½ |
| Free | Ginger, ground. (See Spices.) ...................... | 25 |
| Free | Ginger, unground. " ...................... | 17½ |
| Free | Ginger Ale...... ...... ...... ...... ......... ...... | 17½ |
| Free | Girandoles, Gasaliers and Gas Fittings................ | 17½ |
| Free | Ginghams. (See Cottons.)...................... | 17½ |
| Free | Glass and Glassware, plate and silvered, stained, painted | |
| Free | or colored............ ...... ...... ...... ...... | 17½ |
| Free | Glass Paper and Glass Cloth ...... ...... ......... | 10 |
| 17½ | Glassware ...... ...... ...... ...... ...... ...... | 17½ |

|                                                                                            | P. C. |
|--------------------------------------------------------------------------------------------|-------|
| Glass, Window and Plain                                                                     | 17½   |
| Globes, when imported by and for use of Colleges, Scientific and Literary Societies, and Schools | Free  |
| Glue                                                                                       | 17½   |
| Goat Hair, unmanufactured                                                                   | Free  |
| Gold, Silver and Electro-plate, manufactured                                               | 17½   |
| Gold and Silver Leaf                                                                        | 17½   |
| Gold Beaters' Brim Moulds and Skins                                                         | Free  |
| Grains of all kinds                                                                         | Free  |
| Grass, Osier, Palm Leaf, Straw, Whalebone or Willow, except Plaits elsewhere mentioned. (See Manufactures.) | 17½ |
| Grass Plaits, Fancy                                                                         | Free  |
| Gravels                                                                                     | Free  |
| Grease and Scraps                                                                           | Free  |
| Grease, Axle                                                                                | 17½   |
| Green Fruits. (See Fruits, Green.)                                                          | 10    |
| Green and Dried Fruits, growth and produce of Newfoundland | Free  |
| Grapes. (See Fruits, Green.)                                                                | 10    |
| Grass—Manilla and Sea Grass                                                                 | Free  |
| Grindstones and Scythe Stones                                                               | 17½   |
| Gum, British                                                                                | Free  |
| Gum Arabic, Chewing, and others not elsewhere specified                                     | 17½   |
| Gums, Sandarac, Mastic and Shellac                                                          | Free  |
| Gum, Copal and Damar                                                                        | Free  |
| Guns, Rifles and Fire Arms of all kinds. (When from United States, entry must be authorized by Depart't.) | 17½ |
| Gunpowder, Nitro Glycerine and Fulminating Powder                                           | 17½   |
| Gunpowder and Explosive Substances, used for blasting                                       | 17½   |
| Gutta Percha, unmanufactured                                                                | Free  |
| Gutta Percha, manufactured                                                                  | 17½   |
| Gypsum or Plaster of Paris, neither ground nor calcined.                                    | Free  |
| Gypsum, ground, not calcined, for agricultural purposes.                                    | Free  |
| Grain, and products thereof, viz.:                                                          |       |
| "      Barley, Oats, Peas and Beans, whole                                                  | Free  |

P. C.

| | | | P. C. |
|---|---|---|---|
| 17½ | Grain, and products thereof, viz.: | | |
| | " | Rye, Indian Corn........................ | Free |
| Free | " | Wheat ................................. | Free |
| 17½ | " | Other ................................. | Free |
| Free | " | Flour of Wheat ........................ | Free |
| 17½ | " | Flour of Rye........................... | Free |
| 17½ | " | Indian Meal........................... | Free |
| Free | " | Oatmeal .............................. | Free |
| Free | " | Meal, all others....................... | Free |

**H**

| | | P. C. |
|---|---|---|
| 17½ | | |
| Free | Hair or Mohair, manufactured............... | 17½ |
| Free | Hair, Human, Angola, Buffalo, Curled, Horse and Hog, | |
| Free | Mohair, Goat and Thibet, unmanufactured........ | Free |
| 17½ | Hair, Curled, used in the manufacture of Sofas, Mattrasses, | |
| 10 | &c. ................................. | Free |
| | Harness and Saddlery of Leather manufacture.......... | 17½ |
| Free | Handles for Tools. (See manufactures of Wood.)...... | 17½ |
| 10 | Harmoniums............................ | 17½ |
| Free | Hay and Straw.......................... | 10 |
| 17½ | Hay, Straw and Bran from B.N.A. Provinces............ | Free |
| Free | Hat Plush, for Hatters' use.................. | 10 |
| 17½ | Hats—Beaver, Silk and Felt .................. | 17½ |
| Free | " Straw, Chip, Grass, or other material............ | 17½ |
| Free | " Caps and Bonnets....................... | 17½ |
| | Heavy or Carbolic Oil, used in the manufacture of Wood | |
| 17½ | Block Pavement, &c...................... | Free |
| 17½ | Hemp, undressed........................ | Free |
| 17½ | Hides................................ | Free |
| Free | Horn and Pelts......................... | Free |
| 17½ | Hops....................5 cents per lb. | |
| Free | Hoes. (See Manufactures.)................. | 17½ |
| Free | Hose and Tubing. (See Manufactures.) .......... | 17½ |
| | Hosiery .............................. | 17½ |
| Free | Horn and Ivory. (See Manufactures.) .......... | 17½ |

B

CUSTOMS TARIFF.

|  | P. C. |
|---|---|
| Horses | 10 |
| Horse Hair, unmanufactured | Free |
| Hoop and Sheet Iron | 5 |
| Hubs. (See Manufactures of Wood.) | 17½ |
| Hydraulic Cement or Marine, ground | 17½ |
| Hydraulic Cement or Marine, unground | Free |

## I

| | |
|---|---|
| Indian Corn and Grain of all kinds | Free |
| Indian Meal | Free |
| Indian Rubber, unmanufactured. (See Caoutchouc.) | Free |
| Indian Rubber, manufactured. (See Manufactures.) | 17½ |
| Indigo | Free |
| Inks of all kinds, except Printing Inks | 17½ |
| Inks, Printing | Free |
| Iron, Pig | Free |
| Iron, viz.: Rod, Bar, Hoop or Sheet | 5 |
| " Scrap, Galvanized | 5 |
| " Puddled in Bars, Blooms and Billets | 5 |
| " in Blooms and Billets, not Puddled | 5 |
| " Bolts and Spikes, Galvanized | 5 |
| " Nails and Spikes, rod, round, flat and square | 5 |
| " Hoop for Tires of Driving Wheels of Locomotives, bent and welded | 10 |
| " Boiler Plates and Rolled Plates | 5 |
| " Canada Plates | 5 |
| " Tinned Plates | 5 |
| " Wire, whether Galvanized or not, except for Wire Rigging | 5 |
| " Railroad Bars, Wrought Iron or Steel Chairs and Fish Plates | Free |
| " Tubes and Piping, when drawn, and otherwise | 17½ |
| " Knees and Riders, Ships' | 5 |
| " Masts or parts of Iron Masts | Free |
| Instruments, Musical, not elsewhere specified | 17½ |

P. C.

| | | P. C. |
|---|---|---|
| 10 | Instruments, Musical, for Bands, for use of Army or Navy | Free |
| Free | Ivory, Bone, Pearl and Horn, manufactured............ | 17½ |
| 5 | Ivory, unmanufactured......................... | Free |
| 17½ | Ivory Nuts.................................. | Free |
| 17½ | Ivory or Bone Dice .... ...................... | 17½ |
| Free | | |

## J

| | | |
|---|---|---|
| | Japanned Tin, Planished Tin and Britannia Metal Ware. | 17½ |
| Free | Jeans. (See Cottons.)............................ | 17½ |
| Free | Jewellery and Watches........................... | 17½ |
| Free | Junk and Oakum................................ | Free |
| 17½ | | |
| Free | | |

## K

| | | |
|---|---|---|
| 17½ | Kelp ......................................... | Free |
| Free | Kyrolite ...................................... | Free |
| Free | Knees and Riders, Iron (Ships')............ ...... | 5 |
| 5 | | |
| 5 | | |

## L

| | | |
|---|---|---|
| 5 | Lard and Tallow.................1 cent per lb.; pkgs. | 17½ |
| 5 | "      "  the produce of Newfoundland.......... | Free |
| 5 | Lakes, Scarlet and Maroon, in Pulp................... | Free |
| | Lampblack ..................................... | 17½ |
| 10 | Lead, Pig...................................... | Free |
| 5 | "   Sheet ................................. | Free |
| 5 | "   Red and White, dry ...................... | Free |
| 5 | "   Sugar of............................... | Free |
| | Leather, viz.: Sheep, Calf, Goat and Chamois Skins..... | 17½ |
| 5 | Leather, or Imitation of Leather..................... | 17½ |
| | Leather, manufactured, viz.: Boots and Shoes.......... | 17½ |
| Free | "       "       Harness and Saddlery...... | 17½ |
| 17½ | Leather, Sole and Upper....................... | 10 |
| 5 | Lemons and Oranges............................ | 10 |
| Free | Lemons, Oranges and Citrons, and Rinds of, in brine for | |
| 17½ | candying....................................... | Free |

P. C.

| | |
|---|---|
| Linen | 17½ |
| Linen Machine Thread | 17½ |
| Linen Thread | 17½ |
| Lines and Twines—Fishing | Free |
| Lime | 17½ |
| Lime and Lemon Juice | 17½ |
| Liquorice Juice and Paste | 17½ |
| Lithographic Stones | Free |
| Lithographed, Printed or Copper Plate Bills, &c | 17½ |
| Litharge | Free |
| Lobsters, Preserved, from Countries other than U S | 17½ |
| " Fresh or Preserved in Cans, from U.S | Free |
| Locks | 17½ |
| Locomotive Engine Frames | 10 |
| " " Axles | 10 |
| " " Hoop, Iron or Steel for tires of wheels, bent and welded | 10 |
| " " Cranks and Crank Axles | 10 |
| " " Crank Pins and Connecting Rods | 10 |
| " " Piston Rods, Guide and Slide Bars | 10 |
| Locomotive and Railway Passenger, Baggage and Freight Cars, running upon any line of road crossing the frontier, so long as Canadian Locomotives and Cars are admitted free under similar circumstances in the United States | Free |
| Locomotive Engines | 17½ |
| Lumber, plank and sawed, of Boxwood, Mahogany, Rosewood, Walnut and Pitch Pine | Free |
| Lumber from Newfoundland | Free |

## M

| | |
|---|---|
| Maccaroni and Vermicelli | 17½ |
| Machinery for Mill and Factories, not manufactured in the Dominion | 10 |
| Machinery, not elsewhere specified | 17½ |

| | P. C. |
|---|---|
| Machine Twist and Silk Twist ........................ | $17\frac{1}{2}$ |
| Machine Linen Thread........................................ | $17\frac{1}{2}$ |
| Mace and Nutmegs............................................ | 25 |
| Malt........................2½ cents per lb.; pkgs. | $17\frac{1}{2}$ |
| Manilla Grass and Sea Grass............................ | Free |
| Manures ............................................ | Free |
| Manufactures of Cashmere................................ | $17\frac{1}{2}$ |
| " " Caoutchouc or Indian Rubber, or of Gutta Percha, Boots and Shoes....... | $17\frac{1}{2}$ |
| " " " Belting ................. | $17\frac{1}{2}$ |
| " " " Clothing................. | $17\frac{1}{2}$ |
| " " " Hose and Tubing........ | $17\frac{1}{2}$ |
| " " " All other............... | $17\frac{1}{2}$ |
| " " Brass.......................................... | $17\frac{1}{2}$ |
| " " Copper.......................................... | $17\frac{1}{2}$ |
| " " Fur, or of which Fur is the principal part | $17\frac{1}{2}$ |
| Manufactures of Gold, Silver, Electro-plate, Argentine, Albata, Nickel and Plated and Gilded Ware, of all kinds, not elsewhere specified..................... | $17\frac{1}{2}$ |
| Manufactures of Hair or Mohair, not elsewhere specified. | $17\frac{1}{2}$ |
| " " Iron and Steel Axes.................. | $17\frac{1}{2}$ |
| " " Cutlery of all kinds .................. | $17\frac{1}{2}$ |
| " " Edge Tools .......................... | $17\frac{1}{2}$ |
| " " Files and Rasps...................... | $17\frac{1}{2}$ |
| " " Hoes, Rakes and Forks............... | $17\frac{1}{2}$ |
| " " Locks ................................ | $17\frac{1}{2}$ |
| " " Screws for Wood .................... | $17\frac{1}{2}$ |
| " " Scythes and Snaths .................. | $17\frac{1}{2}$ |
| " " Spades and Shovels.................. | $17\frac{1}{2}$ |
| " " Spikes, Nails, Jacks, Brads and Sprigs.. | $17\frac{1}{2}$ |
| " " Stoves and all other Castings.......... | $17\frac{1}{2}$ |
| " " Surgical Instruments................ | $17\frac{1}{2}$ |
| " " All other............................ | $17\frac{1}{2}$ |
| " " Lead, viz.: Shot, Piping, &c.......... | $17\frac{1}{2}$ |
| " " Leather, viz.: Boots and Shoes......... | $17\frac{1}{2}$ |
| " " " Harness and Saddlery.... | $17\frac{1}{2}$ |

P. C.

Manufactures of Marble or Imitation of Marble, or other
         than rough slabs or blocks ......... 17½
     "        " Papier Maché ..................... 17½
     "        " Pewter, Platina, Japanned and Planished
                  Tin, Britannia Metal Ware, &c....... 17½
     "        " Slate, viz.: Chimney Pieces, Mantles,
                  Pencils, Roofing Slate, prepared ..... 17½
     "        " Stone, not elsewhere specified......... 17½
     "        " Metal and Metal Composition, not else-
                  where specified................... 17½
Marble, unwrought....................................... Free
Masts, iron, or part of Iron Masts (Ships') ............. Free
Maps, Charts and Atlasses.............................. 17½
Meats and Vegetables, preserved....................... 17½
Meats, fresh, salted or smoked......1 cent per lb.; pkgs. 17½
Meats, fresh, salted or smoked, from Newfoundland..... Free
Medals and Gems, and Cabinets of do., including Antiqui-
      ties, Coins, &c..................................... Free
Medicinal Roots in their natural state................. Free
Medicines, Patent...................................... 25
Metal Type, in blocks or pigs.......................... Free
     "     Yellow, in bolts and bars..................... Free
     "        "     for sheathing......................... Free
Metallic Oxides and Ochres, dry, ground or unground,
      washed or unwashed, not calcined ............... Free
Melado........ 25 per cent ad val. and ⅞ths of 1c. per lb.
Military Clothing, imported by Officers of Army or Navy
      stationed in Canada.............................. Free
Millinery of all kinds ................................ 17½
Mineral and Aerated Waters ......... ................. 17½
Mineralogy Specimens.................................. Free
Models, when they cannot be used as the articles of which
      they are said to be the Models .................. Free
Molasses for Refining purposes......73 cents per 100 lbs.
     "     other than for Refining purposes.........ad val. 25
Moss for Upholstery purposes ......................... Free

P. C.

| | | P. C. |
|---|---|---|
| | Mowing, Reaping and Threshing Machines ............ | 17½ |
| 17½ | Musical Instruments for Bands for Army or Navy ....... | Free |
| 17½ | "         "      not elsewhere specified........... | 17½ |
| | Music, Sheet........................................ | 17½ |
| 17½ | Music, Bound. (See Printed Works.) ................ | 5 |
| | Musical Clocks..................................... | 17½ |
| 17½ | Mustard............................................ | 17½ |
| 17½ | | |

## N

| | | |
|---|---|---|
| 17½ | Nails, Tacks and Brads............................. | 17½ |
| Free | Nails, composition................................. | Free |
| Free | Nails, sheathing................................... | Free |
| 17½ | Nail and Spike Rod Iron, round, square or flat ........ | 5 |
| 17½ | Naptha................7½ cents per Imp. gal. ; pkgs. | 17½ |
| 17½ | Natural History, Specimens of...................... | Free |
| Free | Naval and Military Stores........................... | Free |
| | Nitre and Saltpetre ....'........................... | Free |
| Free | Nitro-Glycerine, Fulminating Powder and Explosive Sub- | |
| Free | stances used for Blasting ........................ | 17½ |
| 25 | Nitrate of Soda ................................... | Free |
| Free | Nuts, Ivory ....................................... | Free |
| Free | Nuts, used chiefly in Dyeing....................... | Free |
| Free | Nuts, others, of all kinds.......................... | 17½ |
| | Nutmegs .......................................... | 25 |
| Free | | |

## O

| | | |
|---|---|---|
| Free | Oatmeal and Flour, or Meal of any Grain.............. | Free |
| 17½ | Oats ............................................. | Free |
| 17½ | Oakum ........................................... | Free |
| Free | Ochres, ground or calcined........................ | 17½ |
| | Ochres—dry, ground or unground, washed or unwashed, | |
| Free | not calcined .................................. | Free |
| | Oils, rectified or prepared : | |
| 25 | "  Castor ..................................... | 17½ |
| Free | "  Flax Seed or Linseed...................... | 17½ |

P. C.

Oils, rectified or prepared :
" Hemp and Rape Seed................................ 17½
" Olive and Salad................................... 17½
" Vegetable, not otherwise specified............... 17½
" Volatile or Essential............................ 17½
Oils of all kinds—Crude—except Whale Oils and others
   elsewhere specified.................................. 17½
Oils—Cocoa Nut, Pine and Palm, in their natural state.. Free
Oil—Heavy or Carbolic.................................. Free
Oil—Coal and Kerosene, Naphta, Benzole and Refined
   Petroleum............7¼ cents per Imp. gal. ; pkgs. 17½
" Products of Petroleum     "          "          "   17½
" Crude, Petroleum....      "          "          "   17½
Oil—Cod Liver, Medicinal Preparations, not elsewhere
   specified............................................ 17½
Oil—Fish, and Fish of all kinds, the produce of the Fish-
   eries of the United States, except Fish of the Inland
   Lakes and of the Rivers falling into them, and except
   Fish preserved in Oil................................ Free
Oil—Whale, in the casks from on ship-board, and in the
   condition in which it was first landed.............,.... Free
Oil—Fish, other....................................... 17½
Oil Cake.............................................. Free
Oil Cloths ........................................... 17½
Oil Paintings and Chromos ............................ 17½
Oil Paintings, by Artists of well known merit, or copies
   of the Old Masters by such Artists.................. Free
Old Tom Gin............ ......$1.20 per Imp. gal.; pkgs. 17½
Opium................................................. 17½
Oranges............................................... 10
Oranges, Citrons and Lemons, and Rinds of, in brine for
   candying ........................................... Free
Organs, Melodeons and Harmoniums...................... 17½
Ordnance Stores....................................... Free
Ores of Metals of all kinds .......................... Free
Osiers or Willow...................................... Free

| | | P. C. |
|---|---|---|
| Oysters, in cans, Fresh, from Countries other than U.S... | | 17½ |
| " Preserved, from Countries other than U.S....... | | 17½ |
| " Fresh, from U.S........... | | Free |
| " Fresh, in cans, from U.S............ | | Free |
| " Shelled, in bulk, from U.S............ | | Free |
| Oxides—Metallic, dry, ground or unground, washed or unwashed, not calcined.............. | | Free |

## P

### PACKAGES.

The value of all Bottles, Flasks, Jars, Demijohns, Carboys, Casks, Hogsheads, Pipes, Barrels, and all other Vessels or Packages manufactured by Tin, Iron, Lead, Zinc, Glass or any other material, and capable of holding Liquids; Crates containing Glass, China, Crockery or Earthenware, and all Packages in which Goods are commonly placed for home consumption, including Cases in which Bottled Spirits, Wines or Malt Liquors are contained, and every Package, being the first receptacle or covering enclosing Goods for purposes of sale, shall in all cases in which they contain Goods subject to an *ad valorem* duty, be taken and held to be a part of the fair market value of such Goods for duty, and when they contain Goods subject to specific duty only, such Packages shall be charged with a duty of Customs of 17½ per cent *ad valorem*, to be computed upon their original cost or value, and all Goods not enumerated in this said Act or any other Act, as charged with any duty of Customs, and not declared free of duty by some unrepealed Act or provision—shall be charged with a duty of Customs of 17½ per cent. *ad valorem*, when imported into Canada or taken out of warehouse for consumption therein; but all Packages not hereinbefore specified, and not specially charged with duty by any unrepealed Act, and being the usual and ordinary Packages in which Goods are packed for exportation, according to the general usage and custom of trade, shall be free of duty.

22nd February, 1877.

| | P. C. |
|---|---|
| Packages of Goods paying specific duties............ ...... | 17½ |
| Paints and Colors.... ......... ...... ........ ....... ... | 17½ |
| Paintings in Oil, by Artists of well known merit, or copies of the Old Masters by such Artists ............. ...... | Free |
| Paintings, in Oil, and Chromos not elsewhere specified .. | 17½ |
| Paper, Writing.... ...... ........... .... ...... ..... | 17½ |
| Paper, Printing ...... ....... ......... ......... ...' | 17½ |
| Paper, Wrapping...... ........................ .. ......... | 17½ |
| Paper, all other...... ...... ...... ...... ........ ....., | 17½ |
| Paper Hangings..... ..... ...................... ...... | 17½ |
| Paper, Union Collar Cloth ....., ..................... | Free |
| Paper, Collar Cloth..... ...... ...... ......... ..... | Free |
| Papier Maché ...... ...... ............ ...... ...... | 17½ |
| Paper, Glass and Glass Cloth.... ..... ............. | 10 |
| Parasols and Umbrellas.... ..... .................... | 17½ |
| Patent Medicine and Medicinal Preparations........ ...... | 25 |
| Paris and Permanent Greens...... ..... ....... ...... | Free |
| Peas ...... ........ ...... ...... ...... ...... ...... | Free |
| Peas, Split..... ...... ...... ...... ...... ...... | 17½ |
| Peaches....... ....... ...... ...... ....... ...... ... | 10 |
| Pepper, ground.... ...... ...... ...... ...... ... | 25 |
| Pepper, unground.... ..... ...... ...... ....... ... | 17½ |
| Pelts, Hides and Horns...... ....... ........ ....... | Free |
| Perfumed Spirits........... $1.80 per Imp. gal. ; pkgs. | 17½ |
| Perfumed Spirits, when in flasks or bottles, not weighing more than 4 oz.—See bottles in Perfumed Spirits... | 25 |
| Perfumery, not elsewhere specified.................... | 25 |
| Perfumed and Fancy Soaps ........................ ...... | 25 |
| Petroleum, Refined or not..7⅕ cents per Imp. gal. ; pkgs. | 17½ |
| Pianos ...... ...... ...... ...... ...... ...... ...... | 17½ |
| Pine and Palm Oils in their natural state..... ........ | Free |
| Pine Apples...... ...... ...... ...... ...... ..... .... | 10 |
| Piping and Tubes of Brass, Copper or Iron..... ....... | 17½ |
| Pickles and Sauces...... ...... ...... ...... ......... | 17½ |
| Pimento, ground.... ...... .... ...... ...... ...... .. | 25 |
| Pimento, unground ...... ..... ...... ...... ...... | 17½ |

P. C.

Pig Iron ...................................................... Free

Pig Lead ...................................................... Free

Pipe Clay ..................................................... Free

Pipes, Tobacco ................................................ 17½

Pitch and Tar ................................................. Free

Plaster of Paris, ground and calcined ........................ 17½

Playing Cards ................................................. 25

Plank and Sawed Lumber, not being of Mahogany, Rosewood, Walnut, Chestnut and Cherry, Pitch Pine, Boxwood, or not imported from B.N.A. Provinces ............. 17½

Plank and Sawed Lumber, of Boxwood, Rosewood, Walnut,
Cherry and Chestnut and Pitch Pine .................... Free

Ploughs and parts thereof ..................................... 17½

Plate—Rolled Iron, Boiler Plate ............................... 5

Plates—Canada ................................................. 5

Plates—Tinned ................................................. 5

Preserved Meats and Poultry ................................... 17½

Printed, Lithographed or Copper Plate Bills, &c ............... 17½

Precipitate of Copper ......................................... Free

Precious Stones, unset ........................................ Free

Printers' Implements, &c., viz. : Presses, Electrotype and
Stereotype Blocks for Printing purposes ............... Free

Printing Ink .................................................. Free

Prints and Engravings ......................................... 17½

Proprietary Medicines, mixed with Spirits of Strong
Waters .................. $1.80 per Imp. gal.; pkgs. 17½

Prunes and Plums. (See Dried Fruits.) ........................ 17½

Prunella—Upper of Ladies' Boots and Shoes .................... 10

Photographic Materials ........................................ 17½

Phosphorous ................................................... Free

Philosophical Instruments and Apparatus for Colleges and
Schools .............................................. Free

Powder—Fulminating Gunpowder, Nitro-Glycerine and
*Explosive Substances used for blasting .............. 17½

Powders—Bleaching ............................................. Free

Poultry (Live) ................................................ 10

p. c.

Potatoes ...................................................... 10
Potash, Bichromate of......................................... Free
Porter, in bottles........... 18 cents per Imp. gal ; pkgs. 17½
Porter, in casks .......... 12 cents per Imp. gal. ; pkgs. 17½
Pewter, Platina, Japanned and Planished Tin, Britannia
    Metal Ware............................................ 17½
Pumps and Pump Gear (Ships' material)................. 5
Plants—Trees and Shrubs, growth of Newfoundland .... Free
Plants—Trees and Shrubs....................................... 10

# R

Rags.......................................................... Free
Railroad Cars—Passenger...................................... 17½
    "    "    Freight...................................... 17½
    "    "    Platform..................................... 17½
Railroad Bars—Iron ......................................... Free
    "    "    Steel ......................................... Free
    "    "    Frogs......................................... Free
Railroad Wrought Iron or Steel Chairs and Fish Plates... Free
Railroad Car Axles........................................... Free
Rape and Hemp Seeds ....................................... 10
Rape and Hemp Oils.......................................... 17½
Raspberry Syrup, not containing Spirits................. 17½
Ratan for Chair Makers and Whip Manufacturers....... Free
Raisins ....................................................... 17½
Rennet ....................................................... Free
Rice........... 1 cent per lb.; large bags, free ; pockets, 17½
Riders and Knees, Iron (Ships') ........................... 5
Rifles, Guns and Fire Arms of all kinds ............... 17½
Rigging, Wire (Ships')...................................... Free
Rinds of Oranges, Citrons and Lemons, imported in brine
    for the purpose of candying ........................... Free
Rosin......................................................... Free
Roots—Medicinal, in their natural state................. Free
Roofing Felt ................................................ 17½

p. c.

| | p. c. |
|---|---|
| Roofing Slate, prepared...... | 17½ |
| Ropes and Cordage...... | 17½ |
| Rubber, manufactured...... | 17½ |
| Rubber, unmanufactured...... | Free |
| Rum......$1.20 per Imp. gal. ; pkgs. | 17½ |
| Rum—Shrub......$1.80 per Imp. gal. ; pkgs. | 17½ |
| Rye...... | Free |

## S

| | |
|---|---|
| Sails, ready-made...... | 17½ |
| Sail-cloth or Canvas (Ships' use)...... | 5 |
| Sal Ammoniac...... | Free |
| Sal Soda...... | Free |
| Salt...... | Free |
| Sand Paper and Sand Cloth...... | 17½ |
| Satin and Fine Washed White...... | Free |
| Satinets...... | 17½ |
| Sausage Casings...... | 17½ |
| Screws, for Wood...... | 17½ |
| Schiedam Schnapps......$1.80 per Imp. gal. ; pkgs. | 17½ |
| Scythes and Snaths...... | 17½ |
| Sea Grass and Manilla Grass...... | Free |
| Seeds, not classed as Cereals...... | 10 |
| Seeds from B.N.A. Provinces...... | Free |
| Settlers' Effects of every description, in actual use...... | Free |
| Sewing Machines, and parts thereof...... | 17½ |
| Scraps, Iron...... | 5 |
| Scraps, Brass...... | Free |
| Shawls...... | 17½ |
| Sheet Music, Printed...... | 17½ |
| Ships' Blocks and Patent Bushes for Blocks...... | 5 |
| " Binnacle Lamps...... | 5 |
| " Bunting...... | 5 |
| " Cables—Hemp or Grass...... | 5 |
| " Compasses...... | 5 |

Left margin column:

p. c.
10
Free
17½
17½

17½
5
Free
10

Free
17½
17½
17½
Free
Free
Free
Free
Free
10
17½
17½
Free
17½
Free
17½
5
17½
Free

Free
Free
Free
17½

P. C.

| | |
|---|---|
| Ships' Cordage | 5 |
| " Dead Eyes | 5 |
| " Dead Lights | 5 |
| " Deck Plugs | 5 |
| " Iron Masts or parts of Iron Masts | Free |
| " Knees, Iron | 5 |
| " Pumps and Pump Gear | 5 |
| " Riders, Iron | 5 |
| " Sail-cloth or Canvas | 5 |
| " Shackles | 5 |
| " Sheaves | 5 |
| " Signal Lamps | 5 |
| " Steering Apparatus | 5 |
| " Travelling Trucks | 5 |
| " Varnish, black and bright | 5 |
| " Wedges | 5 |
| " Wire Rigging | Free |
| Shell, manufactured | 17½ |
| Sheet Iron | 5 |
| Shovels | 17½ |
| Shrubs, Trees and Plants | 10 |
| " " " from B.N.A. Provinces | Free |
| Silks, Satins and Velvets | 17½ |
| Silk, Woolen, Worsted and Cotton Embroideries and Tambour Work | 17½ |
| Silk Twist and Machine Twist | 17½ |
| Silk, raw, or as reeled from the Cocoon | Free |
| Silver Coin, United States | 17½ |
| Silver Leaf | 17½ |
| Silver and Gold Cloth | 17½ |
| Silver Plated Ware | 17½ |
| Silver, German Sheet | Free |
| Silicate of Soda | Free |
| Slate, unwrought | Free |
| Slate, manufactured | 17½ |
| Slotted Tapes for the manufacture of Hoop Skirts | Free |

p. c.

| | p. c. |
|---|---|
| Small Wares..................................... | 17½ |
| Snuff, ground, dry.............. 25 cents per lb. and | 12½ |
| Snuff, damp, moist or pickled....... 25 cents per lb. and | 12½ |
| Soda Ash....................................... | Free |
| Soda, Caustic.................................. | Free |
| Soda, Nitrate of .............................. | Free |
| Soap, Common.............. 1 cent per lb.; pkgs. | 17½ |
| Soap, Perfumed and Fancy...................... | 25 |
| Soap, Castile ................................. | 17½ |
| Spades ....................................... | 17½ |
| Spikes and Nails .............................. | 17½ |
| Stoves ....................................... | 17½ |
| Spelter or Zinc, in sheets, blocks or pig.............. | Free |
| Specimens of Natural History, Mineralogy, Botany or Sculpture ..................... | Free |
| Spices, ground, including Ginger, Pimento and Pepper.. | 25 |
| Spices, unground, " " " " .. | 17½ |
| Spikes and Nails, composition.................... | Free |
| Spirits, including Alcohol ....$1.20 per Imp. gal.; pkgs. | 17½ |
| " " Brandy......$1.20 " " " | 17½ |
| " " Cordials ....$1.80 " " " | 17½ |
| " " Gin........$1.20 " " " | 17½ |
| " " Rum ......$1.20 " " " | 17½ |
| Spirits, including Tinctures, Essences and Extracts, $1.80 per Imp. gal.; pkgs. | 17½ |
| " " Whiskey....$1.20 " " " | 17½ |
| " " Others......$1.80 " " " | 17½ |
| Spirits of Turpentine........................... | 17½ |
| Sponges ...................................... | 17½ |
| Starch ....................2 cents per lb.; pkgs. | 17½ |
| Statues of Marble, Bronze and Alabaster, natural size.... | Free |
| Stationery ................................... | 17½ |
| Steam Engines, other than Locomotives.............. | 17½ |
| Steel, wrought or cast, in bars and rods.............. | Free |
| Steel Plates, cut to any form, but not moulded.......... | Free |
| Steel Chairs, Railway.......................... | Free |

Left margin column (p. c.):

5
5
5
5
Free
5
5
5
5
5
5
5
5
5
5
Free
17½
5
17½
10
Free
17½

17½
17½
Free
17½
17½
17½
17½
Free
Free
Free
17½
Free

| | P. C. |
|---|---|
| Steering Apparatus for Ships........................... | 5 |
| Stereotype Blocks for Printing purposes............... | Free |
| Steamboats' and Mill Shafts and Cranks, forged in the rough............................................. | Free |
| Steam Fire Engines................................... | 17½ |
| Stone, unwrought..................................... | Free |
| Stones for Lithographers ............................. | Free |
| Straw................................................ | 10 |
|     "   from the B.N.A. Provinces.................... | Free |
|     "   Tuscan, Grass and Fancy Plaits................. | Free |
| Sulphur of Brimstone, in roll or flour................. | Free |
| Sulphuric Acid....................½ cent per lb.; pkgs. | 17½ |
|     "      "   carboys containing................... | 17½ |
| Sugar Candy, brown or white......1 cent per lb.; ad val. | 25 |
| Sugar, above No. 13 ...............1   "     "     " | 25 |
|   "   equal to or above No. 9....1   "     "     " | 25 |
|   "   below of No 9.............¾   "     "     " | 25 |
| Surgical Instruments.................................. | 17½ |
| Syrup of Sugar or of Sugar Cane, Syrup of Molasses or of Sorghum, Melado, concentrated Melado, or concentrated Melado or Cane Juice, ⅝ cents per lb. and ad val. | 25 |

## T

| | |
|---|---|
| Tafia....................$1.80 per Imp. gal.; pkgs. | 17½ |
| Tails, undressed...................................... | Free |
| Tallow.......................1 cent per lb., pkgs. | 17½ |
| Tampico, white and black............................. | Free |
| Tanners' Bark........................................ | Free |
| Tapes, Slotted, for the manufacture of Hoop Skirts...... | Free |
| Tar and Pitch........................................ | Free |
| Tea, Green and Japan ................6 cents per lb. | |
| Tea, Black .........................5 cents per lb. | |
| Teasels ............................................. | Free |
| Thibet Hair, unmanufactured.......................... | Free |
| Thread, Linen........................................ | 17½ |

P. C.

| | | P. C. |
|---|---|---|
| 5 | Thread, all other | 17½ |
| Free | Thread and other articles embroidered with gold, or for | |
| | embroidery | 17½ |
| Free | Thread Lace and Insertions | 17½ |
| 17½ | Tiles, Drain | Free |
| Free | Timber and Lumber from B.N.A. Provinces | Free |
| Free | Tin, in bar, blocks, pig or granulated | Free |
| 10 | Tin and Zinc or Spelter, in block or pig | Free |
| Free | Tin Clasps, Slides or Spangles, for manufacturing Hoop | |
| Free | Skirts | Free |
| Free | Tin Plates | 5 |
| 17½ | Tinctures containing Spirits .. $1.80 per Imp. gal. ; pkgs. | 17½ |
| 17½ | Tobacco Pipes | 17½ |
| 25 | Tobacco, manufactured.........25 cts. per lb. and *ad val.* | 12½ |
| 25 | Snuff and Snuff Flour.......25  "   "   "   " | 12½ |
| 25 | Snuff, damp, moist or pickled.25  "   "   "   " | 12½ |
| 25 | Tobacco Leaf, unmanufactured (but must be bonded on | |
| 17½ | importation)..: | Free |
| | Tow, undressed | Free |
| | Toys | 17½ |
| 25 | Trees, Shrubs, Roots and Plants | 10 |
| | "    "    "    " from B.N.A. Provinces .. | Free |
| | Travellers' Baggage | Free |
| | "   Carriages.—See Carriages of Travellers | Free |
| i. 17½ | Travelling Trucks (Ships') | 5 |
| . Free | Treenails | Free |
| i. 17½ | Tubes and Piping of Iron | 17½ |
| . Free | "   "   "   Brass | 17½ |
| . Free | "   "   "   Copper | 17½ |
| . Free | Turpentine, Spirits of | 17½ |
| . Free | "   other than Spirits of | Free |
| ). | Type Metal, in blocks or Pigs | Free |
| ). | Type | 5 |
| . Free | | |
| . Free | **U** | |
| . 17½ | Union Collar Cloth Paper | Free |

# V

| | |
|---|---|
| Varnish, bright and black (Ships' use) | 5 |
| Varnish, other than bright and black | 17½ |
| Veneering of Wood | Free |
| Veneering of Ivory | Free |
| Vegetables, including Potatoes and other Roots | 10 |
| Vegetables from B.N.A. Provinces | Free |
| Vegetable Fibres | Free |
| Vegetables used chiefly in Dyeing | Free |
| Velvets, Silks and Satins | 17½ |
| Velveteens | 17½ |
| Vinegar and Acetic Acid...12 cents per Imp. gal. ; pkgs. | 17½ |
| Vitriol, Blue | Free |

# W

| | |
|---|---|
| Walnuts. (Dried Nuts) | 17½ |
| Walnut Lumber—Plank and Sawed | Free |
| Wearing Apparel—Woollen or Cotton | 17½ |
| Weaving or Tram Silk, and Weaving or Tram Cotton, for making elastic webbing, and crinoline thread for covering crinoline wire | Free |
| Water—Cologne in flasks or bottles, not weighing more than 4 ounces | 25 |
| Water—Cologne, others......$1.80 per Imp. gal. ; pkgs. | 17½ |
| Wedges, Ships' | 5 |
| Wax—Bees', Parafine and others | 17½ |
| Wax Candles | 17½ |
| Watches, and parts of | 17½ |
| Warp, Cotton, not coarser than No. 40 | 17½ |
| Whale Oil in the casks, from on Ship-board, and in the condition in which it was first landed | Free |
| Whalebone. (See Manufactures.) | 17½ |
| Wheat | Free |
| Wheat Flour | Free |

P. C.

| | |
|---|---|
| Whiting or Whitening.................................... | Free |
| White Zinc, dry....................................... | Free |
| White Lead, dry...................................... | Free |
| Whiskey. (See Spirits.)......$1.20 per Imp. gal.; pkgs. | 17½ |
| Wick—Cotton Candle................................... | Free |
| Willow or Osiers, unmanufactured...................... | Free |
| Willow and Whalebone. (See Manufactures.)........... | 17½ |
| Wines not containing over 20 degrees of Alcohol, and not worth more than 48 cents per Imp. gal., of all kinds, including Ginger, Orange, Lemon, Goosebarry, Raspberry, Strawberry, Elder and Currant Wine, 6 quarts or 12 pints to the gal..36 cents per Imp. gal.; pkgs. | 17½ |
| Wines, all other when in wood, 72 "    "    "    " | 17½ |
| Wines, all other, except Sparkling, in bottles, 6 quarts or 12 pints to the Imp. gal.......$1.50 per doz.; pkgs. | 17½ |
| Wines, Sparkling................$3 00 per doz.; pkgs. | 17½ |
| Wire Cloth of Brass or Copper......................... | Free |
| Wire—Brass or Copper, round or flat.................. | Free |
| Wire, Iron........................................... | 5 |
| Wire, flat or round, for Crinolines, uncovered.......... | Free |
| Wire, flat, for Crinolines, covered.................... | 17½ |
| Window Glass........................................ | 17½ |
| Wire Rigging (Ships')................................ | Free |
| Wire, Galvanized (Ships')............................ | Free |
| Woods of all kinds, wholly unmanufactured........... | Free |
| Woods, manufactured, not elsewhere specified.......... | 17½ |
| Woods and Drugs used chiefly in dyeing, unmanufactured | Free |
| Wool Waste.......................................... | Free |
| Wool, Cotton......................................... | Free |
| Wool, Raw........................................... | Free |
| Woollen, Worsted and Cotton Embroideries and Tambour Work ........................................ | ½ |
| Woollens, viz. : Blankets, Carpets and Flannels.. | 17½ |
| "              Tweeds, Clothing or Wearing Apparel... | 17½ |
| "              Worsted and Yarn.................... | 17½ |
| "              All others......................... | 17½ |

P. C.

Woollen Netting for India Rubber Shoes and Gloves.....    10
Wrapping Paper.............................................    17½
Writing Paper.............................................    17½
Writing Desks.   (See Fancy Goods.)................    17½
Worsted and Yarns....................................    17½

# Y

Yellow Metal, in bolts and bars......................    Free
   "        "     for Sheathing......................    Free

# Z

Zinc, in sheets, blocks and pigs......................    Free

---

## SPECIAL EXEMPTIONS FROM DUTY.

Apparel, Wearing, of British subjects, dying abroad but domiciled
   in Canada.
Articles imported by and for the use of the Governor-General.
Articles for the public uses of the Dominion.
Articles for the public uses of the Foreign Consuls General.
Army and Navy,                          for the use of.
   "        "      Arms                          "        "
   "        "      Clothing                      "        "
   "        "      Musical instruments for Bands     "        "
   "        "      Military Stores                "        "
Settlers' Effects of every description, in actual use, not being
   merchandise, brought by persons making oath that they
   intend becoming permanent settlers within the Dominion.

## UNDER REGULATIONS AND RESTRICTIONS TO BE PRESCRIBED BY THE MINISTER OF CUSTOMS.

Carriages of Travellers, and Carriages laden with merchandise,
   and not to include Circus Troupes nor Hawkers.
   comotives and Railway, Passenger, Baggage and Freight
   Cars, running upon any line of road crossing the Frontier,
   long as Canadian.

Locomotives and Cars are admitted free under similar circumstances in the United States.

Menageries, Horses, Cattle, Carriages, and Harness of.

Travellers' Baggage.

## SCHEDULE D.

The following Goods, when the growth and produce of any of the British North American Provinces, may be imported free of duty, subject to alteration or regulation, by proclamation of the Governor in Council, viz.:

Animals of all kinds.

Fresh, Smoked and Salted Meats.

Green and Dried Fruits.

Fish of all kinds.

Products of Fish, and of all other creatures living in water.

Poultry, Butter, Cheese, Lard, Tallow, Timber and Lumber of all kinds, round, hewed, but not otherwise manufactured, in whole or in part.

Fish Oil.

Gypsum, ground or unground.

Hay, Hops, Straw, Bran, Seeds of all kinds.

Vegetables, including Potatoes and other Roots.

Plants, Trees and Shrubs.

Coal and Coke.

Salt.

Wheat, Peas and Beans.

Barley, Rye, Oats, Indian Corn, Buckwheat, and all other Grain.

Flour of Wheat and Rye, Indian Meal and Oatmeal, and Flour or Meal of any other Grain.

## SCHEDULE E.

The following articles are prohibited under a penalty of 200 Dollars and forfeiture of Packages in which same may be found, viz.:

Books, Printed Papers, Paintings, Drawings, Prints and Photographs of a treasonable, immoral, seditious or indecent character.

Coin, base or counterfeit.

## EXCISE DUTIES.

On every wine gallon of Spirits of the strength of proof by
    Syke's hydrometer........................................$0.90
On every pound of Malt................................ 0.02
On every gallon of any fermented beverage made in imita-
    tion of Beer or Malt Liquor, and brewed in whole or
    in part from any other substance than Malt.......... 0.08
On Cavendish Tobacco, on any lb. or less quantity....... 0.20
On Canada Twist (*Tabac blanc en torquette*)   do.   ....... 0.10
On Snuff, per lb. or less quantity ..................... 0.20
On all other descriptions of manufactured Tobacco, per lb.
    or less quantity.................................. 0.20
Cigars, (subject to an abatement or allowance for moisture
    in calculating the weight for duty, be fixed by Order
    in Council)...............................40c. per lb.

All goods manufactured in Bond shall, if taken out of Bond
for consumption in Canada, be subject to duties of Excise equal
to the duties of Customs to which they would be subject if imported from Great Britain and entered for consumption in Canada;
and whenever any article, not the produce of Canada, upon
which a duty of Excise would be levied if produced in Canada,
is taken into a Bonded Manufactory, the difference between the
duty of Excise to which it would be so liable and the Customs
duty which would be levied on such article, if imported and
entered for consumption, shall be paid as a duty of Excise when
it is taken into the Bonded Manufactory.

# LIST OF WAREHOUSING PORTS IN THE DOMINION.

## PROVINCE OF QUEBEC.

| | | |
|---|---|---|
| Coaticooke, | Percé, | St. Hyacinthe, |
| Gaspé, | Quebec, | St. Johns, |
| Magdalen Islands, | Rimouski, | Three Rivers. |
| Montreal, | Sherbrooke, | |
| New Carlisle, | Sorel, | |

## PROVINCE OF ONTARIO.

| | | |
|---|---|---|
| Amherstburg, | Elgin (Edwardsb'g), | Paris, |
| Belleville, | Fort Erie, | Peterboro', |
| Brantford, | Galt, | Picton, |
| Brockville, | Gananoque, | Port Hope, |
| Chatham, | Guelph, | Prescott, |
| Chippewa, | Hamilton, | Prince Arth's Land'g, |
| Clifton, | Kincardine, | Sarnia, |
| Cobourg, | Kingston, | St. Catherines, |
| Colborne (Welland | Lindsay, | Sault Ste. Marie, |
| Canal), | London, | Stanley, |
| Collingwood, | Morrisburg, | Stratford, |
| Cornwall, | Napanee, | Toronto, |
| Cramahe, | Newcastle, | Trenton, |
| Darlington (Bow- | Niagara, | Wallaceburg, |
| manville), | Oakville, | Whitby, |
| Dover, | Oshawa, | Windsor, |
| Dundas, | Owen Sound, | Woodstock. |
| Dunnville, | Ottawa, | |

## PROVINCE OF NEW BRUNSWICK.

| | | |
|---|---|---|
| Bathurst, | Hillsborough, | St. George, |
| Caraquette, | Moncton, | St. John, |
| Chatham, | Newcastle, | St. Stephens, |
| Dalhousie, | Richibucton, | West Isles, |
| Dorchester, | Sackville, | Woodstock. |
| Frederickton, | Shediac, | |
| Grand Falls, | St. Andrews, | |

## PROVINCE OF NOVA SCOTIA.

Amherst,
Annapolis,
Antigonish,
Arichat,
Baddeck,
Barrington,
Bridgetown,
Cornwallis,
Digby,
Guysboro',

Halifax,
Liverpool,
Locke Port,
Londonderry,
Lunenburg,
Margaretsville,
North Sydney,
Parrsborough,
Pictou,
Port Hawkesbury,

Port Hood,
Port Medway,
Shelburne,
Sydney,
Truro,
Weymouth,
Windsor,
Yarmouth,

## PROVINCE OF BRITISH COLUMBIA.
Victoria.

## PROVINCE OF MANITOBA.
Winnipeg.

## PROVINCE OF PRINCE EDWARD ISLAND.
Charlottetown.

# TABLE

SHEWING THE

## VALUE IN DOLLARS AND CENTS

OF ALL

## Sums from One Penny to Fifty Thousand Pounds Stg.

CALCULATED

### AT 9½, OR NEW PAR OF EXCHANGE.

| £ | $ c. | £ | $ c. | £ | $ c. |
|---|---|---|---|---|---|
| 1... | 4.87 | 21... | 102.20 | 41... | 199.53 |
| 2... | 9.73 | 22... | 107.07 | 42... | 204.40 |
| 3... | 14.60 | 23... | 111.93 | 43... | 209.27 |
| 4... | 19.47 | 24... | 116.80 | 44... | 214.13 |
| 5... | 24.33 | 25... | 121.67 | 45... | 219.00 |
| 6... | 29.20 | 26... | 126.53 | 46... | 223.87 |
| 7... | 34.07 | 27... | 131.40 | 47... | 228.73 |
| 8... | 38.93 | 28... | 136.27 | 48... | 233.60 |
| 9... | 43.80 | 29... | 141.13 | 49... | 238.47 |
| 10... | 48.67 | 30... | 146.00 | 50... | 243.33 |
| 11... | 53.53 | 31... | 150.87 | 51... | 248.20 |
| 12... | 58.40 | 32... | 155.73 | 52... | 253.07 |
| 13... | 63.27 | 33... | 160.60 | 53... | 257.93 |
| 14... | 68.13 | 34... | 165.47 | 54... | 262.80 |
| 15... | 73.00 | 35... | 170.33 | 55.. | 267.67 |
| 16... | 77.87 | 36... | 175.20 | 56... | 272.53 |
| 17... | 82.73 | 37... | 180.07 | 57... | 277.40 |
| 18... | 87.60 | 38... | 184.93 | 58... | 282.27 |
| 19... | 92.47 | 39... | 189.80 | 59... | 287.13 |
| 20... | 97.33 | 40... | 194.67 | 60... | 292.00 |

| £ | $ c. | £ | $ c. | £ | $ c. |
|---|------|---|------|---|------|
| 61.. | 296.87 | 98... | 476.93 | 135... | 657.00 |
| 62... | 301.72 | 99... | 481.80 | 136... | 661.87 |
| 63... | 306.60 | 100... | 486.67 | 137... | 666.73 |
| 64... | 311.47 | 101... | 491.53 | 138... | 671.60 |
| 65... | 316.33 | 102... | 496.40 | 139... | 676.47 |
| 66... | 321.20 | 103... | 501.27 | 140... | 681.33 |
| 67... | 326.07 | 104... | 506.13 | 141... | 686.20 |
| 68... | 330.93 | 105... | 511.00 | 142... | 691.07 |
| 69... | 335.80 | 106... | 515.87 | 143... | 695.93 |
| 70... | 340.67 | 107... | 520.73 | 144... | 700.80 |
| 71... | 345.53 | 108... | 525.60 | 145... | 705.67 |
| 72... | 350.40 | 109... | 530.47 | 146... | 710.53 |
| 73... | 355.27 | 110... | 535.33 | 147... | 715.40 |
| 74... | 360.13 | 111... | 540.20 | 148... | 720.27 |
| 75... | 365.00 | 112... | 545.07 | 149... | 725.13 |
| 76... | 369.87 | 113... | 549.93 | 150... | 730.00 |
| 77... | 374.73 | 114... | 554.80 | 151... | 734.87 |
| 78... | 379.60 | 115... | 559.67 | 152... | 739.73 |
| 79... | 384.47 | 116... | 564.53 | 153... | 744.60 |
| 80... | 389.33 | 117... | 569.40 | 154... | 749.47 |
| 81... | 394.20 | 118... | 574.27 | 155... | 754.33 |
| 82... | 399.07 | 119... | 579.13 | 156... | 759.20 |
| 83... | 403.93 | 120... | 584.00 | 157... | 764.07 |
| 84... | 408.80 | 121... | 588.87 | 158... | 768.93 |
| 85... | 413.67 | 122... | 593.73 | 159... | 773.80 |
| 86... | 418.53 | 123... | 598.60 | 160... | 778.67 |
| 87... | 423.40 | 124... | 603.47 | 161... | 783.53 |
| 88... | 428.27 | 125... | 608.33 | 162... | 788.40 |
| 89... | 433.13 | 126... | 613.20 | 163... | 793.27 |
| 90... | 438.00 | 127... | 618.07 | 164... | 798.13 |
| 91... | 442.87 | 128... | 622.93 | 165... | 803.00 |
| 92... | 447.73 | 129... | 627.80 | 166... | 807.87 |
| 93... | 452.60 | 130... | 632.67 | 167... | 812.73 |
| 94... | 457.47 | 131... | 637.53 | 168... | 817.60 |
| 95... | 462.33 | 132... | 642.40 | 169... | 822.47 |
| 96... | 467.20 | 133... | 647.27 | 170... | 827.33 |
| 97... | 472.07 | 134... | 652.13 | 171... | 832.20 |

| £ | $ c. | £ | $ c. | £ | $ c. |
|---|---|---|---|---|---|
| 172... | 837.07 | 209... | 1017.13 | 246... | 1197.20 |
| 173... | 841.93 | 210... | 1022.00 | 247... | 1202.07 |
| 174... | 846.80 | 211... | 1026.87 | 248... | 1206.93 |
| 175... | 851.67 | 212... | 1031.73 | 249... | 1211.80 |
| 176... | 856.53 | 213... | 1036.60 | 250... | 1216.67 |
| 177... | 861.40 | 214... | 1041.47 | 251... | 1221.53 |
| 178... | 866.27 | 215... | 1046.33 | 252... | 1226.40 |
| 179... | 871.13 | 216... | 1051.20 | 253... | 1231.27 |
| 180... | 876.00 | 217... | 1056.07 | 254... | 1236.13 |
| 181... | 880.87 | 218... | 1060.93 | 255... | 1241.00 |
| 182... | 885.73 | 219... | 1065.80 | 256... | 1245.87 |
| 183... | 890.60 | 220... | 1070.67 | 257... | 1250.73 |
| 184... | 895.47 | 221... | 1075.53 | 258... | 1255.60 |
| 185... | 900.33 | 222... | 1080.40 | 259... | 1260.47 |
| 186... | 905.20 | 223... | 1085.27 | 260... | 1265.33 |
| 187... | 910.07 | 224... | 1090.13 | 261... | 1270.20 |
| 188... | 914.93 | 225... | 1095.00 | 262... | 1275.07 |
| 189... | 919.80 | 226... | 1099.87 | 263... | 1279.93 |
| 190... | 924.67 | 227... | 1104.73 | 264... | 1284.80 |
| 191... | 929.53 | 228... | 1109.60 | 265... | 1289.67 |
| 192... | 934.40 | 229... | 1114.47 | 266... | 1294.53 |
| 193... | 939.27 | 230... | 1119.33 | 267... | 1299.40 |
| 194... | 944.13 | 231... | 1124.20 | 268... | 1304.27 |
| 195... | 949.00 | 232... | 1129.07 | 269... | 1309.13 |
| 196... | 953.87 | 233... | 1133.93 | 270... | 1314.00 |
| 197... | 958.73 | 234... | 1138.80 | 271... | 1318.87 |
| 198... | 963.60 | 235... | 1143.67 | 272... | 1323.73 |
| 199... | 968.47 | 236... | 1148.53 | 273... | 1328.60 |
| 200... | 973.33 | 237... | 1153.40 | 274... | 1333.47 |
| 201... | 978.20 | 238... | 1158.27 | 275... | 1338.33 |
| 202... | 983.07 | 239... | 1163.13 | 276... | 1343.20 |
| 203... | 987.93 | 240... | 1168.00 | 277... | 1348.07 |
| 204... | 992.80 | 241... | 1172.87 | 278... | 1352.93 |
| 205... | 997.67 | 242... | 1177.73 | 279... | 1357.80 |
| 206... | 1002.53 | 243... | 1182.60 | 280... | 1362.67 |
| 207... | 1007.40 | 244... | 1187.47 | 281... | 1367.53 |
| 208... | 1,012.27 | 245... | 1192.33 | 282... | 1372.40 |

44

| £ | $ c. | £ | $ c. | £ | $ c. | £ |
|---|---|---|---|---|---|---|
| 283 | 1377.27 | 320 | 1557.33 | 357 | 1737.40 | 394 |
| 284 | 1382.13 | 321 | 1562.20 | 358 | 1742.27 | 395 |
| 285 | 1387.00 | 322 | 1567.07 | 359 | 1747.13 | 396 |
| 286 | 1391.87 | 323 | 1571.93 | 360 | 1752.00 | 397 |
| 287 | 1396.73 | 324 | 1576.80 | 361 | 1756.87 | 398 |
| 288 | 1401.60 | 325 | 1581.67 | 362 | 1761.73 | 399 |
| 289 | 1406.47 | 326 | 1586.53 | 363 | 1766.60 | 400 |
| 290 | 1411.33 | 327 | 1591.40 | 364 | 1771.47 | 401 |
| 291 | 1416.20 | 328 | 1596.27 | 365 | 1776.33 | 402 |
| 292 | 1421.07 | 329 | 1601.13 | 366 | 1781.20 | 403 |
| 293 | 1425.93 | 330 | 1606.00 | 367 | 1786.07 | 404 |
| 294 | 1430.80 | 331 | 1610.87 | 368 | 1790.93 | 405 |
| 295 | 1435.67 | 332 | 1615.73 | 369 | 1795.80 | 406 |
| 296 | 1440.53 | 333 | 1620.60 | 370 | 1800.67 | 407 |
| 297 | 1445.40 | 334 | 1625.47 | 371 | 1805.53 | 408 |
| 298 | 1450.27 | 335 | 1630.33 | 372 | 1810.40 | 409 |
| 299 | 1455.13 | 336 | 1635.20 | 373 | 1815·27 | 410 |
| 300 | 1460.00 | 337 | 1640.07 | 374 | 1820.13 | 411 |
| 301 | 1464.87 | 338 | 1644.93 | 375 | 1825.00 | 412 |
| 302 | 1469.73 | 339 | 1649.80 | 376 | 1829.87 | 413 |
| 303 | 1474.60 | 340 | 1654.67 | 377 | 1834.73 | 414 |
| 304 | 1479.47 | 341 | 1659.53 | 378 | 1839.60 | 415 |
| 305 | 1484.33 | 342 | 1664.40 | 379 | 1844.47 | 416 |
| 306 | 1489.20 | 343 | 1669.27 | 380 | 1849.33 | 417 |
| 307 | 1494.07 | 344 | 1674.13 | 381 | 1854 20 | 418 |
| 308 | 1498.93 | 345 | 1679.00 | 382 | 1859.07 | 419 |
| 309 | 1503.80 | 346 | 1683.87 | 383 | 1863.93 | 420 |
| 310 | 1508.67 | 347 | 1688.73 | 384 | 1868.80 | 421 |
| 311 | 1513.53 | 348 | 1693.60 | 385 | 1873.67 | 422 |
| 312 | 1518.40 | 349 | 1698.47 | 386 | 1878.53 | 423 |
| 313 | 1523.27 | 350 | 1703.33 | 387 | 1883.40 | 424 |
| 314 | 1528.13 | 351 | 1708.20 | 388 | 1888.27 | 425 |
| 315 | 1533.00 | 352 | 1713.07 | 389 | 1893.13 | 426 |
| 316 | 1537.87 | 353 | 1717.93 | 390 | 1898.00 | 427 |
| 317 | 1542.73 | 354 | 1722.80 | 391 | 1902.87 | 428 |
| 318 | 1547.60 | 355 | 1727.67 | 392 | 1907.73 | 429 |
| 319 | 1552.47 | 356 | 1732.53 | 393 | 1912.60 | 430 |

| £ | $ c. | £ | $ c. | £ | $ c. |
|---|------|---|------|---|------|
| 394... | 1917.47 | 431... | 2097.53 | 468... | 2277.60 |
| 395... | 1922.33 | 432... | 2102.40 | 469... | 2282.47 |
| 396... | 1927.20 | 433... | 2107.27 | 470... | 2287.33 |
| 397... | 1932.07 | 434... | 2112.13 | 471... | 2292.20 |
| 398... | 1936.93 | 435... | 2117.00 | 472... | 2297.07 |
| 399... | 1941.80 | 436... | 2121.87 | 473... | 2301.93 |
| 400... | 1946.67 | 437... | 2126.73 | 474... | 2306.80 |
| 401... | 1951.53 | 438... | 2131.60 | 475... | 2311.67 |
| 402... | 1956.40 | 439... | 2136.47 | 476... | 2316.53 |
| 403... | 1961.27 | 440... | 2141.33 | 477... | 2321.40 |
| 404... | 1966.13 | 441... | 2146.20 | 478... | 2326.27 |
| 405... | 1971.00 | 442... | 2151.07 | 479... | 2331.13 |
| 406... | 1975.87 | 443... | 2155.93 | 480... | 2336.00 |
| 407... | 1980.73 | 444... | 2160.80 | 481... | 2340.87 |
| 408... | 1985.60 | 445... | 2165.67 | 482... | 2345.73 |
| 409... | 1990.47 | 446... | 2170.53 | 483... | 2350.60 |
| 410... | 1995.33 | 447... | 2175.40 | 484... | 2355.47 |
| 411... | 2000.20 | 448... | 2180.27 | 485... | 2360.33 |
| 412... | 2005.07 | 449... | 2185.13 | 486... | 2365.20 |
| 413... | 2009.93 | 450... | 2190.00 | 487... | 2370.07 |
| 414... | 2014.80 | 451... | 2194.87 | 488... | 2374.93 |
| 415... | 2019.67 | 452... | 2199.73 | 489... | 2379.80 |
| 416... | 2024.53 | 453... | 2204.60 | 490... | 2384.67 |
| 417... | 2029.40 | 454... | 2209.47 | 491... | 2389.53 |
| 418... | 2034.27 | 455... | 2214.33 | 492... | 2394.40 |
| 419... | 2039.13 | 456... | 2219.20 | 493... | 2399.27 |
| 420... | 2044.00 | 457... | 2224.07 | 494... | 2404.13 |
| 421... | 2048.87 | 458... | 2228.93 | 495... | 2409.00 |
| 422... | 2053.73 | 459... | 2233.80 | 496... | 2413.87 |
| 423... | 2058.60 | 460... | 2238.67 | 497... | 2418.73 |
| 424... | 2063.47 | 461... | 2243.53 | 498... | 2423.60 |
| 425... | 2068.33 | 462... | 2248.40 | 499... | 2428.47 |
| 426... | 2073.20 | 463... | 2253.27 | 500... | 2433.33 |
| 427... | 2078.07 | 464... | 2258.13 | 501... | 2438.20 |
| 428... | 2082.93 | 465... | 2263.00 | 502... | 2443.07 |
| 429... | 2087.80 | 466... | 2267.87 | 503... | 2447.93 |
| 430... | 2092.67 | 467... | 2272.73 | 504... | 2452.80 |

| £ | $ | c. | £ | $ | c. | £ | $ | c. |
|---|---|---|---|---|---|---|---|---|
| 505... | 2457 | .67 | 542... | 2637 | .73 | 579... | 2817 | .80 |
| 506... | 2462 | .53 | 543... | 2642 | .60 | 580... | 2822 | .67 |
| 507... | 2467 | .40 | 544... | 2647 | .47 | 581... | 2827 | .53 |
| 508... | 2472 | .27 | 545.. | 2652 | .33 | 582... | 2832 | .40 |
| 509... | 2477 | .13 | 546... | 2657 | .20 | 583... | 2837 | .27 |
| 510... | 2482 | .00 | 547... | 2662 | .07 | 584... | 2842 | .13 |
| 511... | 2486 | .87 | 548... | 2666 | .93 | 585... | 2847 | .00 |
| 512... | 2491 | .73 | 549... | 2671 | .80 | 586... | 2851 | .87 |
| 513... | 2496 | .60 | 550... | 2676 | .67 | 587... | 2856 | .73 |
| 514... | 2501 | .47 | 551... | 2681 | .63 | 588... | 2861 | .60 |
| 515... | 2506 | .33 | 552... | 2686 | .40 | 589... | 2866 | .47 |
| 516... | 2511 | .20 | 553... | 2691 | .27 | 590... | 2871 | .33 |
| 517... | 2516 | .07 | 554... | 2696 | .13 | 591... | 2876 | .20 |
| 518... | 2520 | .93 | 555... | 2701 | .00 | 592... | 2881 | .07 |
| 519... | 2525 | .80 | 556... | 2705 | .87 | 593... | 2885 | .93 |
| 520... | 2530 | .67 | 557... | 2710 | .73 | 594... | 2890 | .80 |
| 521... | 2535 | .53 | 558... | 2715 | .60 | 595... | 2895 | .67 |
| 522... | 2540 | .40 | 559... | 2720 | .47 | 596... | 2900 | .53 |
| 523... | 2545 | .27 | 560... | 2725 | .33 | 597... | 2905 | .40 |
| 524... | 2550 | .13 | 561... | 2730 | .20 | 598... | 2910 | .27 |
| 525... | 2555 | .00 | 562... | 2735 | .07 | 599... | 2915 | .13 |
| 526... | 2559 | .87 | 563... | 2739 | .93 | 600... | 2920 | .00 |
| 527... | 2564 | .73 | 564... | 2744 | .80 | 601... | 2924 | .87 |
| 528... | 2569 | .60 | 565... | 2749 | .67 | 602... | 2929 | .73 |
| 529... | 2574 | .47 | 566... | 2754 | .53 | 603... | 2934 | .60 |
| 530... | 2579 | .33 | 567... | 2759 | .40 | 604... | 2939 | .47 |
| 531... | 2584 | .20 | 568... | 2764 | .27 | 605... | 2944 | .33 |
| 532... | 2589 | .07 | 569... | 2769 | .13 | 606... | 2949 | .20 |
| 533... | 2593 | .93 | 570... | 2774 | .00 | 607... | 2954 | .07 |
| 534... | 2598 | .80 | 571... | 2778 | .87 | 608... | 2958 | .93 |
| 535... | 2603 | .67 | 572... | 2783 | .73 | 609... | 2963 | .80 |
| 536... | 2608 | .53 | 573... | 2788 | .60 | 610... | 2968 | .67 |
| 537... | 2613 | .40 | 574... | 2793 | .46 | 611... | 2973 | .53 |
| 538... | 2618 | .27 | 575... | 2798 | .33 | 612... | 2978 | .40 |
| 539... | 2623 | .13 | 576... | 2803 | .20 | 613... | 2983 | .27 |
| 540... | 2628 | .00 | 577... | 2808 | .07 | 614... | 2988 | .13 |
| 541... | 2632 | .87 | 578... | 2812 | .93 | 615... | 2993 | .00 |

| £ | $ c. | £ | $ c. | £ | $ c. |
|---|------|---|------|---|------|
| 616 | 2997.87 | 653 | 3177.93 | 690 | 3358.00 |
| 617 | 3002.73 | 654 | 3182.80 | 691 | 3362.87 |
| 618 | 3007.60 | 655 | 3187.67 | 692 | 3367.73 |
| 619 | 3012.47 | 656 | 3192.53 | 693 | 3372.60 |
| 620 | 3017.33 | 657 | 3197.40 | 694 | 3377.47 |
| 621 | 3022.20 | 658 | 3202.27 | 695 | 3382.33 |
| 622 | 3027.07 | 659 | 3207.13 | 696 | 3387.20 |
| 623 | 3031.93 | 660 | 3212.00 | 697 | 3392.07 |
| 624 | 3036.80 | 661 | 3216.87 | 698 | 3396.93 |
| 625 | 3041.67 | 662 | 3221.73 | 699 | 3401.80 |
| 626 | 3046.53 | 663 | 3226.60 | 700 | 3406.67 |
| 627 | 3051.40 | 664 | 3231.47 | 701 | 3411.53 |
| 628 | 3056.27 | 665 | 3236.33 | 702 | 3416.40 |
| 629 | 3061.13 | 666 | 3241.20 | 703 | 3421.27 |
| 630 | 3066.00 | 667 | 3246.07 | 704 | 3426.13 |
| 631 | 3070.87 | 668 | 3250.93 | 705 | 3431.00 |
| 632 | 3075.73 | 669 | 3255.80 | 706 | 3435.87 |
| 633 | 3080.60 | 670 | 3260.67 | 707 | 3440.73 |
| 634 | 3085.47 | 671 | 3265.53 | 708 | 3445.60 |
| 635 | 3090.33 | 672 | 3270.40 | 709 | 3450.47 |
| 636 | 3095.20 | 673 | 3275.27 | 710 | 3455.33 |
| 637 | 3100.07 | 674 | 3280.13 | 711 | 3460.20 |
| 638 | 3104.93 | 675 | 3285.00 | 712 | 3465.07 |
| 639 | 3109.80 | 676 | 3289.87 | 713 | 3469.93 |
| 640 | 3114.67 | 677 | 3294.73 | 714 | 3474.80 |
| 641 | 3119.53 | 678 | 3299.60 | 715 | 3479.67 |
| 642 | 3124.40 | 679 | 3304.47 | 716 | 3484.53 |
| 643 | 3129.27 | 680 | 3309.33 | 717 | 3489.40 |
| 644 | 3134.13 | 681 | 3314.20 | 718 | 3494.27 |
| 645 | 3139.00 | 682 | 3319.07 | 719 | 3499.13 |
| 646 | 3143.87 | 683 | 3323.93 | 720 | 3504.00 |
| 647 | 3148.73 | 684 | 3328.80 | 721 | 3508.87 |
| 648 | 3153.60 | 685 | 3333.67 | 722 | 3513.73 |
| 649 | 3158.47 | 686 | 3338.53 | 723 | 3518.60 |
| 650 | 3163.33 | 687 | 3343.40 | 724 | 3523.47 |
| 651 | 3168.20 | 688 | 3348.27 | 725 | 3528.33 |
| 652 | 3173.07 | 689 | 3353.13 | 726 | 3533.20 |

| C | $ | c. | C | $ | c. | C | $ | c |
|---|---|---|---|---|---|---|---|---|
| 727... | 3538.07 | | 764... | 3718.13 | | 801... | 3898.20 | |
| 728... | 3542.93 | | 765... | 3723.00 | | 802... | 3903.07 | |
| 729... | 3547.80 | | 766... | 3727.87 | | 803... | 3907.93 | |
| 730... | 3552.67 | | 767... | 3732.73 | | 804... | 3912.80 | |
| 731... | 3557.53 | | 768... | 3737.60 | | 805... | 3917.67 | |
| 732... | 3562.40 | | 769... | 3742.47 | | 806... | 3922.53 | |
| 733... | 3567.27 | | 770... | 3747.33 | | 807... | 3927.40 | |
| 734... | 3572.13 | | 771... | 3752.20 | | 808... | 3932.27 | |
| 735... | 3577.00 | | 772... | 3757.07 | | 809... | 3937.13 | |
| 736... | 3581.87 | | 773... | 3761.93 | | 810... | 3942.00 | |
| 737... | 3586.73 | | 774... | 3766.80 | | 811... | 3946.87 | |
| 738... | 3591.60 | | 775... | 3771.67 | | 812... | 3951.73 | |
| 739... | 3596.47 | | 776... | 3776.53 | | 813... | 3956.60 | |
| 740... | 3601.33 | | 777... | 3781.40 | | 814... | 3961.47 | |
| 741... | 3606.20 | | 778... | 3786.27 | | 815... | 3966.33 | |
| 742... | 3611.07 | | 779... | 3791.13 | | 816... | 3971.20 | |
| 743... | 3615.93 | | 780... | 3796.00 | | 817... | 3976.07 | |
| 744... | 3620.80 | | 781... | 3800.87 | | 818... | 3980.93 | |
| 745... | 3625.67 | | 782... | 3805.73 | | 819... | 3985.80 | |
| 746... | 3630.53 | | 783... | 3810.60 | | 820... | 3990.67 | |
| 747... | 3635.40 | | 784... | 3815.47 | | 821... | 3995.53 | |
| 748... | 3640.27 | | 785... | 3820.33 | | 822... | 4000.40 | |
| 749... | 3645.13 | | 786... | 3825.20 | | 823... | 4005.27 | |
| 750... | 3650.00 | | 787... | 3830.07 | | 824... | 4010.13 | |
| 751... | 3654.87 | | 788... | 3834.93 | | 825... | 4015.00 | |
| 752... | 3659.73 | | 789... | 3839.80 | | 826... | 4019.87 | |
| 753... | 3664.60 | | 790... | 3844.67 | | 827... | 4024.73 | |
| 754... | 3669.47 | | 791... | 3849.53 | | 828... | 4029.60 | |
| 755... | 3674.33 | | 792... | 3854.40 | | 829... | 4034.47 | |
| 756... | 3679.20 | | 793... | 3859.27 | | 830... | 4039.33 | |
| 757... | 3684.07 | | 794... | 3864.13 | | 831... | 4044.20 | |
| 758... | 3688.93 | | 795... | 3869.00 | | 832... | 4049.07 | |
| 759... | 3693.80 | | 796... | 3873.87 | | 833... | 4053.93 | |
| 760... | 3698.67 | | 797... | 3878.73 | | 834... | 4058.80 | |
| 761... | 3703.53 | | 798... | 3883.60 | | 835... | 4063.67 | |
| 762... | 3708.40 | | 799... | 3888.47 | | 836... | 4068.53 | |
| 763... | 3713.27 | | 800... | 3893.33 | | 837... | 4073.40 | |

| £ | $ c. | £ | $ c. | £ | $ c. |
|---|---|---|---|---|---|
| 838 | 4078.27 | 875 | 4258.33 | 912 | 4438.40 |
| 839 | 4083.13 | 876 | 4263.20 | 913 | 4443.27 |
| 840 | 4088.00 | 877 | 4268.07 | 914 | 4448.13 |
| 841 | 4092.87 | 878 | 4272.93 | 915 | 4453.00 |
| 842 | 4097.73 | 879 | 4277.80 | 916 | 4457.87 |
| 843 | 4102.60 | 880 | 4282.67 | 917 | 4462.73 |
| 844 | 4107.47 | 881 | 4287.53 | 918 | 4467.60 |
| 845 | 4112.33 | 882 | 4292.40 | 919 | 4472.47 |
| 846 | 4117.20 | 883 | 4297.27 | 920 | 4477.33 |
| 847 | 4122.07 | 884 | 4302.13 | 921 | 4482.20 |
| 848 | 4126.93 | 885 | 4307.00 | 922 | 4487.07 |
| 849 | 4131.80 | 886 | 4311.87 | 923 | 4491.93 |
| 850 | 4136.67 | 887 | 4316.73 | 924 | 4496.80 |
| 851 | 4141.53 | 888 | 4321.60 | 925 | 4501.67 |
| 852 | 4146.40 | 889 | 4326.47 | 926 | 4506.53 |
| 853 | 4151.27 | 890 | 4331.33 | 927 | 4511.40 |
| 854 | 4156.13 | 891 | 4336.20 | 928 | 4516.27 |
| 855 | 4161.00 | 892 | 4341.07 | 929 | 4521.13 |
| 856 | 4165.87 | 893 | 4345.93 | 930 | 4526.00 |
| 857 | 4170.73 | 894 | 4350.80 | 931 | 4530.87 |
| 858 | 4175.60 | 895 | 4355.67 | 932 | 4535.73 |
| 859 | 4180.47 | 896 | 4360.53 | 933 | 4540.60 |
| 860 | 4185.33 | 897 | 4365.40 | 934 | 4545.47 |
| 861 | 4190.20 | 898 | 4370.27 | 935 | 4550.33 |
| 862 | 4195.07 | 899 | 4375.13 | 936 | 4555.20 |
| 863 | 4199.93 | 900 | 4380.00 | 937 | 4560.07 |
| 864 | 4204.80 | 901 | 4384.87 | 938 | 4564.93 |
| 865 | 4209.67 | 902 | 4389.73 | 939 | 4569.80 |
| 866 | 4214.53 | 903 | 4394.60 | 940 | 4574.67 |
| 867 | 4219.40 | 904 | 4399.47 | 941 | 4579.53 |
| 868 | 4224.27 | 905 | 4404.33 | 942 | 4584.40 |
| 869 | 4229.13 | 906 | 4409.20 | 943 | 4589.27 |
| 870 | 4234.00 | 907 | 4414.07 | 944 | 4594.13 |
| 871 | 4238.87 | 908 | 4418.93 | 945 | 4599.00 |
| 872 | 4243.73 | 909 | 4423.80 | 946 | 4603.84 |
| 873 | 4248.60 | 910 | 4428.67 | 947 | 4608.73 |
| 874 | 4253.47 | 911 | 4433.53 | 948 | 4613.60 |

| £ | $ c. | £ | $ c. | £ | $ c. |
|---|---|---|---|---|---|
| 949... | 4618.47 | 973... | 4735.27 | 997... | 4852.07 |
| 950... | 4623.33 | 974... | 4740.13 | 998... | 4856.93 |
| 951... | 4628.20 | 975... | 4745.00 | 999... | 4861.80 |
| 952... | 4633.07 | 976... | 4749.87 | 1000... | 4866.67 |
| 953... | 4637.93 | 977... | 4754.73 | 1100... | 5353.33 |
| 954... | 4642.80 | 978... | 4759.60 | 1200... | 5840.00 |
| 955... | 4647.67 | 979... | 4764.47 | 1300... | 6326.67 |
| 956... | 4652.53 | 980... | 4769.33 | 1400... | 6813.33 |
| 957... | 4657.40 | 981... | 4774.20 | 1500... | 7300.00 |
| 958... | 4662.27 | 982... | 4779.07 | 1600... | 7786.67 |
| 959... | 4667.13 | 983... | 4783.93 | 1700... | 8273.33 |
| 960... | 4672.00 | 984... | 4788.80 | 1800... | 8760.00 |
| 961... | 4676.87 | 985... | 4793.67 | 1900... | 9246.67 |
| 962... | 4681.73 | 986... | 4798.53 | 2000... | 9733.33 |
| 963... | 4686.60 | 987... | 4803.40 | 3000... | 14600.00 |
| 964... | 4691.47 | 988... | 4808.27 | 4000... | 19466.67 |
| 965... | 4696.33 | 989... | 4813.13 | 5000... | 24333.33 |
| 966... | 4701.20 | 990... | 4818.00 | 6000... | 29200.00 |
| 967... | 4706.07 | 991... | 4822.87 | 7000... | 34066.67 |
| 968... | 4710.93 | 992... | 4827.73 | 8000... | 38933.33 |
| 969... | 4715.80 | 993... | 4832.60 | 9000... | 43800.00 |
| 970... | 4720.67 | 994... | 4837.47 | 10000... | 48666.67 |
| 971... | 4725.53 | 995... | 4842.33 | 50000... | 243333.33 |
| 972... | 4730.40 | 996... | 4847.20 | | |

| PENCE. | | SHILLINGS. | | SHILLINGS. | |
|---|---|---|---|---|---|
| 1... | 2.1–12 | 1... | $.24\frac{1}{3}$ | 13... | $3.16\frac{1}{3}$ |
| 2... | 4.1–6 | 2... | $.48\frac{2}{3}$ | 14... | $3.40\frac{2}{3}$ |
| 3... | 6.1–4 | 3... | .73 | 15... | 3.65 |
| 4... | 8.1–3 | 4... | $.97\frac{1}{3}$ | 16... | $3.89\frac{1}{3}$ |
| 5... | 10.5–12 | 5... | $1.21\frac{2}{3}$ | 17... | $4.13\frac{2}{3}$ |
| 6... | 12.1–2 | 6... | 1.46 | 18... | 4.38 |
| 7... | 14.7–12 | 7... | $1.70\frac{1}{3}$ | 19... | 4.62 |
| 8... | 16.2–3 | 8... | $1.94\frac{2}{3}$ | 20... | $4.86\frac{2}{3}$ |
| 9... | 18.3–4 | 9... | 2.19 | | |
| 10... | 20.5–6 | 10... | $2.43\frac{1}{3}$ | | |
| 11... | 22.11-12 | 11... | $2.67\frac{2}{3}$ | | |
| 12... | 25 | 12... | 2.92 | | |

# FRANCS

### REDUCED TO

# DOLLARS AND CENTS.

—•—

## 1 FRANC EQUAL TO 19⅖ CENTS.

• ◀◆▶ •

| F. | $ c. | F. | $ c. | F. | $ c. |
|----|------|----|------|----|------|
| 1... | .19 | 25... | 4.83 | 49... | 9.46 |
| 2... | .39 | 26... | 5.02 | 50... | 9.65 |
| 3... | .58 | 27... | 5.21 | 51... | 9.84 |
| 4... | .77 | 28... | 5.40 | 52... | 10.04 |
| 5... | .97 | 29... | 5.60 | 53... | 10.23 |
| 6... | 1.16 | 30... | 5.79 | 54... | 10.42 |
| 7... | 1.35 | 31... | 5.98 | 55... | 10.62 |
| 8... | 1.54 | 32... | 6.18 | 56... | 10.81 |
| 9... | 1.74 | 33... | 6.37 | 57... | 11.00 |
| 10... | 1.93 | 34... | 6.56 | 58... | 11.19 |
| 11... | 2.12 | 35... | 6.76 | 59... | 11.39 |
| 12... | 2.32 | 36... | 6.95 | 60... | 11.58 |
| 13... | 2.51 | 37... | 7.14 | 61... | 11.77 |
| 14... | 2.70 | 38... | 7.33 | 62... | 11.97 |
| 15... | 2.90 | 39... | 7.53 | 63... | 12.16 |
| 16... | 3.09 | 40... | 7.72 | 64... | 12.35 |
| 17... | 3.28 | 41... | 7.91 | 65... | 12.55 |
| 18... | 3.47 | 42... | 8.11 | 66... | 12.74 |
| 19... | 3.67 | 43... | 8.30 | 67... | 12.93 |
| 20... | 3.86 | 44... | 8.49 | 68... | 13.12 |
| 21... | 4.05 | 45... | 8.69 | 69... | 13.32 |
| 22... | 4.25 | 46... | 8.88 | 70... | 13.51 |
| 23... | 4.44 | 47... | 9.07 | 71... | 13.70 |
| 24... | 4.63 | 48... | 9.26 | 72... | 13.90 |

| F. | $ c. | F. | $ c. | F. | $ c. |
|---|---|---|---|---|---|
| 73... | 14.09 | 110... | 21.23 | 147... | 28.37 |
| 74... | 14.28 | 111... | 21.42 | 148... | 28.56 |
| 75... | 14.48 | 112... | 21.62 | 149... | 28.76 |
| 76... | 14.67 | 113... | 21.81 | 150... | 28.95 |
| 77... | 14.86 | 114... | 22.00 | 151... | 29.14 |
| 78... | 15.05 | 115... | 22.20 | 152... | 29.34 |
| 79... | 15.25 | 116... | 22.39 | 153... | 29.53 |
| 80... | 15.44 | 117... | 22.58 | 154... | 29.72 |
| 81... | 15.63 | 118... | 22.77 | 155... | 29.92 |
| 82... | 15.83 | 119... | 22.97 | 156... | 30.11 |
| 83... | 16.02 | 120... | 23.16 | 157... | 30.30 |
| 84... | 16.21 | 121... | 23.35 | 158... | 30.49 |
| 85... | 16.41 | 122... | 23.55 | 159... | 30.69 |
| 86... | 16.60 | 123... | 23.74 | 160... | 30.88 |
| 87... | 16.79 | 124... | 23.93 | 161... | 31.07 |
| 88... | 16.98 | 125... | 24.13 | 162... | 31.27 |
| 89... | 17.18 | 126... | 24.32 | 163... | 31.46 |
| 90... | 17.37 | 127... | 24.51 | 164... | 31.65 |
| 91... | 17.56 | 128... | 24.70 | 165... | 31.85 |
| 92... | 17.76 | 129... | 24.90 | 166... | 32.04 |
| 93... | 17.95 | 130... | 25.09 | 167... | 32.23 |
| 94... | 18.14 | 131... | 25.28 | 168... | 32.42 |
| 95... | 18.34 | 132... | 25.48 | 169... | 32.62 |
| 96... | 18.53 | 133... | 25.67 | 170... | 32.81 |
| 97... | 18.72 | 134... | 25.86 | 171... | 33.00 |
| 98... | 18.91 | 135... | 26.06 | 172... | 33.20 |
| 99... | 19.11 | 136... | 26.25 | 173... | 33.39 |
| 100... | 19.30 | 137... | 26.44 | 174... | 33.58 |
| 101... | 19.49 | 138... | 26.63 | 175... | 33.78 |
| 102... | 19.69 | 139... | 26.83 | 176... | 33.97 |
| 103... | 19.88 | 140... | 27.02 | 177... | 34.16 |
| 104... | 20.07 | 141... | 27.21 | 178... | 34.35 |
| 105... | 20.27 | 142... | 27.41 | 179... | 34.55 |
| 106... | 20.46 | 143... | 27.60 | 180... | 34.74 |
| 107... | 20.65 | 144... | 27.79 | 181... | 34.93 |
| 108... | 20.84 | 145... | 27.99 | 182... | 35.13 |
| 109... | 21.04 | 146... | 28.18 | 183... | 35.32 |

| F. | $ c. | F. | $ c. | F. | $ c. |
|---|---|---|---|---|---|
| 184... | 35.51 | 221... | 42.65 | 258... | 49.79 |
| 185... | 35.71 | 222... | 42.85 | 259... | 49.99 |
| 186... | 35.90 | 223... | 43.04 | 260... | 50.18 |
| 187... | 36.09 | 224... | 43.23 | 261... | 50.37 |
| 188... | 36 28 | 225... | 43.43 | 262... | 50.57 |
| 189... | 36.48 | 226... | 43.62 | 263... | 50.76 |
| 190... | 36.67 | 227... | 43.81 | 264... | 50.95 |
| 191... | 36.86 | 228... | 44.00 | 265... | 51.15 |
| 192... | 37.06 | 229... | 44.20 | 266... | 51.34 |
| 193... | 37.25 | 230... | 44.39 | 267... | 51.53 |
| 194... | 37.44 | 231... | 44.58 | 268... | 51.72 |
| 195... | 37.64 | 232... | 44.78 | 269... | 51.92 |
| 196... | 37.83 | 233... | 44.97 | 270... | 52.11 |
| 197... | 38.02 | 234... | 45.16 | 271... | 52.30 |
| 198... | 38.21 | 235... | 45.36 | 272... | 52.50 |
| 199... | 38.41 | 236... | 45.55 | 273... | 52.69 |
| 200... | 38.60 | 237... | 45.74 | 274... | 52.88 |
| 201.. | 38.79 | 238.. | 45.93 | 275... | 53.08 |
| 202... | 38.99 | 239... | 46.13 | 276... | 53.27 |
| 203... | 39.18 | 240... | 46.32 | 277... | 53.46 |
| 204... | 39.37 | 241... | 46.51 | 278... | 53.65 |
| 205... | 39.57 | 242... | 46.71 | 279... | 53.85 |
| 206... | 39.76 | 243... | 46.90 | 280... | 54.04 |
| 207... | 39.95 | 244... | 47.09 | 281... | 54.23 |
| 208... | 40.14 | 245... | 47.29 | 282... | 54.43 |
| 209... | 40.34 | 246... | 47.48 | 283... | 54.62 |
| 210... | 40.53 | 247... | 47.67 | 284... | 54.81 |
| 211... | 40.72 | 248... | 47.86 | 285... | 55.01 |
| 212... | 40.92 | 249... | 48.06 | 286... | 55.20 |
| 213... | 41.11 | 250... | 48.25 | 287... | 55.39 |
| 214... | 41.30 | 251... | 48.44 | 288... | 55.58 |
| 215... | 41.50 | 252... | 48.64 | 289... | 55.78 |
| 216... | 41.69 | 253... | 48.83 | 290... | 55.97 |
| 217... | 41.88 | 254... | 49.02 | 291... | 56.16 |
| 218... | 42.07 | 255... | 49.22 | 292... | 56.36 |
| 219... | 42.27 | 256... | 49.41 | 293... | 56.55 |
| 220... | 42.46 | 257... | 49.60 | 294... | 56.74 |

| F. | $ c. | F. | $ c. | F. | $ c. |
|---|---|---|---|---|---|
| 295... | 56.94 | 332... | 64.08 | 369... | 71.22 |
| 296... | 57.13 | 333... | 64.27 | 370... | 71.41 |
| 297... | 57.32 | 334... | 64.46 | 371... | 71.60 |
| 298... | 57.51 | 335... | 64.66 | 372... | 71.80 |
| 299... | 57.71 | 336... | 64.85 | 373... | 71.99 |
| 300... | 57.90 | 337... | 65.04 | 374... | 72.18 |
| 301... | 58.09 | 338... | 65.23 | 375... | 72.38 |
| 302... | 58.29 | 339... | 65.43 | 376... | 72.57 |
| 303... | 58.48 | 340... | 65.62 | 377... | 72.76 |
| 304... | 58.67 | 341... | 65.81 | 378... | 72.95 |
| 305... | 58.87 | 342... | 66.01 | 379... | 73.15 |
| 306... | 59.06 | 343... | 66.20 | 380... | 73.34 |
| 307... | 59.25 | 344... | 66.39 | 381... | 73.53 |
| 308... | 59.44 | 345... | 66.59 | 382... | 73.73 |
| 309... | 59.64 | 346... | 66.78 | 383... | 73.92 |
| 310... | 59.83 | 347... | 66.97 | 384... | 74.11 |
| 311... | 60.02 | 348... | 67.16 | 385... | 74.31 |
| 312... | 60.22 | 349... | 67.36 | 386... | 74.50 |
| 313... | 60.41 | 350... | 67.55 | 387... | 74.69 |
| 314... | 60.60 | 351... | 67.74 | 388... | 74.88 |
| 315... | 60.80 | 352... | 67.94 | 389... | 75.08 |
| 316... | 60.99 | 353... | 68.13 | 390... | 75.27 |
| 317... | 61.18 | 354... | 68.32 | 391... | 75.46 |
| 318... | 61.37 | 355... | 68.52 | 392... | 75.66 |
| 319... | 61.57 | 356... | 68.71 | 393... | 75.85 |
| 320... | 61.76 | 357... | 68.90 | 394... | 76.04 |
| 321... | 61.95 | 358... | 69.09 | 395... | 76.24 |
| 322... | 62.15 | 359... | 69.29 | 396... | 76.43 |
| 323... | 62.34 | 360... | 69.48 | 397... | 76.62 |
| 324... | 62.53 | 361... | 69.67 | 398... | 76.81 |
| 325... | 62.73 | 362... | 69.87 | 399... | 77.01 |
| 326... | 62.92 | 363... | 70.06 | 400... | 77.20 |
| 327... | 63.11 | 364... | 70.25 | 401... | 77.39 |
| 328... | 63.30 | 365... | 70.45 | 402... | 77.59 |
| 329... | 63.50 | 366... | 70.64 | 403... | 77.78 |
| 330... | 63.69 | 367... | 70.83 | 404... | 77.97 |
| 331... | 63.88 | 368... | 71.02 | 405... | 78.17 |

| F. | $ C. | F. | $ C. | F. | $ C. |
|---|---|---|---|---|---|
| 406 | 78.36 | 443 | 85.50 | 480 | 92.64 |
| 407 | 78.55 | 444 | 85.69 | 481 | 92.83 |
| 408 | 78.74 | 445 | 85.89 | 482 | 93.03 |
| 409 | 78.94 | 446 | 86.08 | 483 | 93.22 |
| 410 | 79.13 | 447 | 86.27 | 484 | 93.41 |
| 411 | 79.32 | 448 | 86.46 | 485 | 93.61 |
| 412 | 79.52 | 449 | 86.66 | 486 | 93.80 |
| 413 | 79.71 | 450 | 86.85 | 487 | 93.99 |
| 414 | 79.90 | 451 | 87.04 | 488 | 94.18 |
| 415 | 80.10 | 452 | 87.24 | 489 | 94.38 |
| 416 | 80.29 | 453 | 87.43 | 490 | 94.57 |
| 417 | 80.48 | 454 | 87.62 | 491 | 94.76 |
| 418 | 80.67 | 455 | 87.82 | 492 | 94.96 |
| 419 | 80.87 | 456 | 88.01 | 493 | 95.15 |
| 420 | 81.06 | 457 | 88.20 | 494 | 95.34 |
| 421 | 81.25 | 458 | 88.39 | 495 | 95.54 |
| 422 | 81.45 | 459 | 88.59 | 496 | 95.73 |
| 423 | 81.64 | 460 | 88.78 | 497 | 95.92 |
| 424 | 81.83 | 461 | 88.97 | 498 | 96.11 |
| 425 | 82.03 | 462 | 89.17 | 499 | 96.31 |
| 426 | 82.22 | 463 | 89.36 | 500 | 96.50 |
| 427 | 82.41 | 464 | 89.55 | 501 | 96.69 |
| 428 | 82.60 | 465 | 89.75 | 502 | 96.89 |
| 429 | 82.80 | 466 | 89.94 | 503 | 97.08 |
| 430 | 82.99 | 467 | 90.13 | 504 | 97.27 |
| 431 | 83.18 | 468 | 90.32 | 505 | 97.47 |
| 432 | 83.38 | 469 | 90.52 | 506 | 97.66 |
| 433 | 83.57 | 470 | 90.71 | 507 | 97.85 |
| 434 | 83.76 | 471 | 90.90 | 508 | 98.04 |
| 435 | 83.96 | 472 | 91.10 | 509 | 98.24 |
| 436 | 84.15 | 473 | 91.29 | 510 | 98.43 |
| 437 | 84.34 | 474 | 91.48 | 511 | 98.62 |
| 438 | 84.53 | 475 | 91.68 | 512 | 98.82 |
| 439 | 84.73 | 476 | 91.87 | 513 | 99.01 |
| 440 | 84.92 | 477 | 92.06 | 514 | 99.20 |
| 441 | 85.11 | 478 | 92.25 | 515 | 99.40 |
| 442 | 85.31 | 479 | 92.45 | 516 | 99.59 |

| F. | $ c. | F. | $ c. | F. | $ c. |
|---|---|---|---|---|---|
| 517 | 99.78 | 554 | 106.92 | 591 | 114.06 |
| 518 | 99.97 | 555 | 107.12 | 592 | 114.26 |
| 519 | 100.17 | 556 | 107.31 | 593 | 114.46 |
| 520 | 100.36 | 557 | 107.50 | 594 | 114.64 |
| 521 | 100.55 | 558 | 107.69 | 595 | 114.84 |
| 522 | 100.75 | 559 | 107.89 | 596 | 115.03 |
| 523 | 100.94 | 560 | 108.08 | 597 | 115.22 |
| 524 | 101 13 | 561 | 108.27 | 598 | 115.41 |
| 525 | 101.33 | 562 | 108.47 | 599 | 115.61 |
| 526 | 101.52 | 563 | 108.66 | 600 | 115.80 |
| 527 | 101.71 | 564 | 108.85 | 601 | 115.99 |
| 528 | 101.90 | 565 | 109.05 | 602 | 116.19 |
| 529 | 102.10 | 566 | 109.24 | 603 | 116.38 |
| 530 | 102.29 | 567 | 109.43 | 604 | 116.57 |
| 531 | 102.48 | 568 | 109.62 | 605 | 116.77 |
| 532 | 102.68 | 569 | 109.82 | 606 | 116.96 |
| 533 | 102.87 | 570 | 110.01 | 607 | 117.15 |
| 534 | 103.06 | 571 | 110.20 | 608 | 117.34 |
| 535 | 103.26 | 572 | 110.40 | 609 | 117.54 |
| 536 | 103.45 | 573 | 110.59 | 610 | 117.73 |
| 537 | 103.64 | 574 | 110.78 | 611 | 117.92 |
| 538 | 103.83 | 575 | 110.98 | 612 | 118.12 |
| 539 | 104.03 | 576 | 111.17 | 613 | 118.31 |
| 540 | 104.22 | 577 | 111.36 | 614 | 118.50 |
| 541 | 104.41 | 578 | 111.55 | 615 | 118.70 |
| 542 | 104.61 | 579 | 111.75 | 616 | 118.89 |
| 543 | 104.80 | 580 | 111.94 | 617 | 119.08 |
| 544 | 104.99 | 581 | 112.13 | 618 | 119.27 |
| 545 | 105.19 | 582 | 112.33 | 619 | 119.47 |
| 546 | 105.38 | 583 | 112.52 | 620 | 119.66 |
| 547 | 105.57 | 584 | 112.71 | 621 | 119.85 |
| 548 | 105.76 | 585 | 112.91 | 622 | 120.05 |
| 549 | 105.96 | 586 | 113.10 | 623 | 120.24 |
| 550 | 106.15 | 587 | 113.29 | 624 | 120.43 |
| 551 | 106.34 | 588 | 113.48 | 625 | 120.63 |
| 552 | 106.54 | 589 | 113.68 | 626 | 120.82 |
| 553 | 106.73 | 590 | 113.87 | 627 | 121.01 |

| F. | $ C. | F. | $ C. | F. | $ C. |
|---|---|---|---|---|---|
| 628... | 121.20 | 665... | 128.35 | 702... | 135.49 |
| 629... | 121.40 | 666... | 128.54 | 703... | 135.68 |
| 630... | 121.59 | 667... | 128.73 | 704... | 135.87 |
| 631... | 121.78 | 668... | 128.92 | 705... | 136.07 |
| 632... | 121.98 | 669... | 129.12 | 706... | 136.26 |
| 633... | 122.17 | 670... | 129.31 | 707... | 136.45 |
| 634... | 122.36 | 671... | 129.50 | 708... | 136.64 |
| 635... | 122.56 | 672... | 129.70 | 709... | 136.84 |
| 636... | 122.75 | 673... | 129.89 | 710... | 137.03 |
| 637... | 122.94 | 674... | 130.08 | 711... | 137.22 |
| 638... | 123.13 | 675... | 130.28 | 712... | 137.42 |
| 639... | 123.33 | 676... | 130.47 | 713... | 137.61 |
| 640... | 123.52 | 677... | 130.66 | 714... | 137.80 |
| 641... | 123.71 | 678... | 130.85 | 715... | 138.00 |
| 642... | 123.91 | 679... | 131.05 | 716... | 138.19 |
| 643... | 124.10 | 680... | 131.24 | 717... | 138.38 |
| 644... | 124.29 | 681... | 131.43 | 718... | 138.57 |
| 645... | 124.49 | 682... | 131.63 | 719... | 138.77 |
| 646... | 124.68 | 683... | 131.82 | 720... | 138.96 |
| 647... | 124.87 | 684... | 132.01 | 721... | 139.15 |
| 648... | 125.06 | 685... | 132.21 | 722... | 139.35 |
| 649... | 125.26 | 686... | 132.40 | 723... | 139.54 |
| 650... | 125.45 | 687... | 132.59 | 724... | 139.73 |
| 651... | 125.64 | 688... | 132.78 | 725... | 139.93 |
| 652... | 125.84 | 689... | 132.98 | 726... | 140.12 |
| 653... | 126.03 | 690... | 133.17 | 727... | 140.31 |
| 654... | 126.22 | 691... | 133.36 | 728... | 140.50 |
| 655... | 126.42 | 692... | 133.56 | 729... | 140.70 |
| 656... | 126.61 | 693... | 133.75 | 730... | 140.89 |
| 657... | 126.80 | 694... | 133.94 | 731... | 141.08 |
| 658... | 126.99 | 695... | 134.14 | 732... | 141.28 |
| 659... | 127.19 | 696... | 134.33 | 733... | 141.47 |
| 660... | 127.38 | 697... | 134.52 | 734... | 141.66 |
| 661... | 127.57 | 698... | 134.71 | 735... | 141.86 |
| 662... | 127.77 | 699... | 134.91 | 736... | 142.05 |
| 663... | 127.96 | 700... | 135.10 | 737... | 142.24 |
| 664... | 128.15 | 701... | 135.29 | 738... | 142.43 |

| F. | $ c. | F. | $ c. | F. | $ c. |
|---|---|---|---|---|---|
| 739... | 142.63 | 776... | 149.77 | 813... | 156.91 |
| 740... | 142.82 | 777... | 149.96 | 814... | 157.10 |
| 741... | 143.01 | 778... | 150.15 | 815... | 157.30 |
| 742... | 143.21 | 779... | 150.35 | 816... | 157.49 |
| 743... | 143.40 | 780... | 150.54 | 817... | 157.68 |
| 744... | 143.59 | 781... | 150.73 | 818... | 157.87 |
| 745... | 143.79 | 782... | 150.93 | 819... | 158.07 |
| 746... | 143.98 | 783... | 151.12 | 820... | 158.26 |
| 747... | 144.17 | 784... | 151.31 | 821... | 158.45 |
| 748... | 144.36 | 785... | 151.51 | 822... | 158.65 |
| 749... | 144.56 | 786... | 151.70 | 823... | 158.84 |
| 750... | 144.75 | 787... | 151.89 | 824... | 159.03 |
| 751... | 144.94 | 788... | 152.08 | 825... | 159.23 |
| 752... | 145.14 | 789... | 152.28 | 826... | 159.42 |
| 753... | 145.33 | 790... | 152.47 | 827... | 159.61 |
| 754... | 145.52 | 791... | 152.66 | 828... | 159.80 |
| 755... | 145.72 | 792... | 152.86 | 829... | 160.00 |
| 756... | 145.91 | 793... | 153.05 | 830... | 160.19 |
| 757... | 146.10 | 794... | 153.24 | 831... | 160.38 |
| 758... | 146.29 | 795... | 153.44 | 832... | 160.58 |
| 759... | 146.49 | 796... | 153.63 | 833... | 160.77 |
| 760... | 146.68 | 797... | 153.82 | 834... | 160.96 |
| 761... | 146.87 | 798... | 154.01 | 835... | 161.16 |
| 762... | 147.07 | 799... | 154·21 | 836... | 161.35 |
| 763... | 147.26 | 800... | 154.40 | 837... | 161.54 |
| 764... | 147.45 | 801... | 154.59 | 838... | 161.73 |
| 765... | 147.65 | 802... | 154.79 | 839... | 161.93 |
| 766... | 147.84 | 803... | 154.98 | 840... | 162.12 |
| 767... | 148.03 | 804... | 155.17 | 841... | 162.31 |
| 768... | 148.22 | 805... | 155.37 | 842... | 162.51 |
| 769... | 148.42 | 806... | 155.56 | 843... | 162.70 |
| 770... | 148.61 | 807... | 155.75 | 844... | 162.89 |
| 771... | 148.80 | 808... | 155.94 | 845... | 163.09 |
| 772... | 149.00 | 809... | 156.14 | 846... | 163.28 |
| 773... | 149.19 | 810... | 156.33 | 847... | 163.47 |
| 774... | 149.38 | 811... | 156.52 | 848... | 163.66 |
| 775... | 149.58 | 812... | 156.72 | 849... | 163.86 |

| F. | $ c. | F. | $ c. | F. | $ c. |
|---|---|---|---|---|---|
| 850 | 164.05 | 887 | 171.19 | 924 | 178.33 |
| 851 | 164.24 | 888 | 171.38 | 925 | 178.53 |
| 852 | 164.44 | 889 | 171.58 | 926 | 178.72 |
| 853 | 164.63 | 890 | 171.77 | 927 | 178.91 |
| 854 | 164.82 | 891 | 171.96 | 928 | 179.10 |
| 855 | 165.02 | 892 | 172.16 | 929 | 179.30 |
| 856 | 165.21 | 893 | 172.35 | 930 | 179.49 |
| 857 | 165.40 | 894 | 172.54 | 931 | 179.68 |
| 858 | 165.59 | 895 | 172.74 | 932 | 179.88 |
| 859 | 165.79 | 896 | 172.93 | 933 | 180.07 |
| 860 | 165.98 | 897 | 173.12 | 934 | 180.26 |
| 861 | 166.17 | 898 | 173.31 | 935 | 180.46 |
| 862 | 166.37 | 899 | 173.51 | 936 | 180.65 |
| 863 | 166.56 | 900 | 173.70 | 937 | 180.84 |
| 864 | 166.75 | 901 | 173.89 | 938 | 181.03 |
| 865 | 166.95 | 902 | 174.09 | 939 | 181.23 |
| 866 | 167.14 | 903 | 174.28 | 940 | 181.42 |
| 867 | 167.33 | 904 | 174.47 | 941 | 181.61 |
| 868 | 167.52 | 905 | 174.67 | 942 | 181.81 |
| 869 | 167.72 | 906 | 174.86 | 943 | 182.00 |
| 870 | 167.91 | 907 | 175.05 | 944 | 182.19 |
| 871 | 168.10 | 908 | 175 24 | 945 | 182.39 |
| 872 | 168.30 | 909 | 175.44 | 946 | 182.58 |
| 873 | 168.49 | 910 | 175.63 | 947 | 182.77 |
| 874 | 168.68 | 911 | 175.82 | 948 | 182.96 |
| 875 | 168.88 | 912 | 176.02 | 949 | 183.16 |
| 876 | 169.07 | 913 | 176.21 | 950 | 183.35 |
| 877 | 169.26 | 914 | 176.40 | 951 | 183.54 |
| 878 | 169.45 | 915 | 176.60 | 952 | 183.74 |
| 879 | 169.65 | 916 | 176.79 | 953 | 183.93 |
| 880 | 169.84 | 917 | 176.98 | 954 | 184.12 |
| 881 | 170.03 | 918 | 177.17 | 955 | 184.32 |
| 882 | 170.23 | 919 | 177.37 | 956 | 184.51 |
| 883 | 170.42 | 920 | 177.56 | 957 | 184.70 |
| 884 | 170.61 | 921 | 177.75 | 958 | 184.89 |
| 885 | 170.81 | 922 | 177.95 | 959 | 185.09 |
| 886 | 171.00 | 923 | 178.14 | 960 | 185.28 |

| F. | $ c. | F. | $ c. | F. | $ c. |
|---|---|---|---|---|---|
| 961... | 185.47 | 983... | 189.72 | 1500... | 289.50 |
| 962... | 185.67 | 984... | 189.91 | 1600... | 308.80 |
| 963... | 185.86 | 985... | 190.11 | 1700... | 328.10 |
| 964... | 186.05 | 986... | 190.30 | 1800... | 347.40 |
| 965... | 186.25 | 987... | 190.49 | 1900... | 366.70 |
| 966... | 186.44 | 988... | 190.68 | 2000... | 386.00 |
| 967... | 136.63 | 989... | 190.88 | 2500... | 482.50 |
| 968... | 186.82 | 990... | 191.07 | 3000... | 579.00 |
| 969... | 187.02 | 991... | 191.26 | 3500... | 675.50 |
| 970... | 187.21 | 992... | 191.46 | 4000... | 772.00 |
| 971... | 187.40 | 993... | 191.65 | 4500... | 868.50 |
| 972... | 187.60 | 994... | 191.84 | 5000... | 965.00 |
| 973... | 187.79 | 995... | 192.04 | 5500... | 1061.50 |
| 974... | 187.98 | 996... | 192.23 | 6000... | 1158.00 |
| 975... | 188.18 | 997... | 192.42 | 6500... | 1254.00 |
| 976... | 188.37 | 998... | 192.61 | 7000... | 1351.00 |
| 977... | 188.56 | 999... | 192.81 | 7500... | 1447.50 |
| 978... | 188.75 | 1000... | 193.00 | 8000... | 1544.00 |
| 979... | 188.95 | 1100... | 212.30 | 8500... | 1640.50 |
| 980... | 189.14 | 1200... | 231.60 | 9000... | 1737.00 |
| 981... | 189.33 | 1300... | 250.90 | 9500... | 1833.50 |
| 982... | 189.53 | 1400... | 270.20 | 10000... | 1930.00 |

Austrian Florin....................45$\frac{6}{10}$ cents.
German Imperial Marks.........23$\frac{8}{10}$ "
Dutch Florins.....................38$\frac{6}{10}$ "
Belgian Francs......... ...........19$\frac{3}{10}$ "
French        "     .................19$\frac{3}{10}$ "

www.ingramcontent.com/pod-product-compliance
Lightning Source LLC
Chambersburg PA
CBHW021634270326
41931CB00008B/1015